Praise fo.

T0267569

"In *Fungal*, Ariel Gordon leads us on an intimate journey through diverse landscapes of mushrooms and the people who love them, from urban to wild, commercial to kitschy. Her blend of wisdom and humour enriches the experience, offering insightful reflections and emotional depth. I loved it! I got lost in new worlds and emerged all the better for it."
– Kim Anderson, author of *A Recognition of Being: Reconstructing Native Womanhood*

"Ariel Gordon's *Fungal: Foraging in the Urban Forest* is a perfect companion for anyone curious about not only mushrooms but the complexities of ecosystems of all kinds, natural and human-made. Every page is animated by wild energy and muddy joy. How lucky we are to have this excellent forager's guide not only to mushrooms and their possibilities (culinary, medicinal, psychotropic) but also to big ideas, to happiness and to community."
– Theresa Kishkan, author of *Blue Portugal and Other Essays*

"Ariel Gordon's *Fungal* is an ecstasy of attention. For over twenty years, she has pored over the urban forest, neighbourhoods, riverbanks and surrounding parklands of her Winnipeg home to celebrate the everyday, everywhere presence of beings at our feet: mushrooms. Her quirky, compelling pursuit of fungi slaps mosquitos, crams in reams of material from the library and the internet, and slogs through muddy back roads as she forages from the days of Selkirk's treaty with Chief Peguis in 1817 to her harvesting alongside Cantonese- or Somali-speaking factory workers in 2021 and onwards to her rummaging with Ukrainian neighbours in flight from the current war with Russia in search of pidpanki honey mushrooms. Ariel Gordon treats readers to the world of wonders in a fungal spore."
– Daniel Coleman, author of *Yardwork: A Biography of an Urban Place*

"Ariel Gordon's complex collection of essays clusters together like a living organism – a fleshy and fruitful species that captures the essence of life, inoculating readers with the succulence of what spawns from moments when we truly pay attention. Revelling in the intricacies of mushroom varieties – those glorious layers of spores – and treasures found in the muck, Gordon focuses a magnifying glass on what is hidden in our ecosystem, and what can be found if we look closely. The essays in *Fungal* are akin to the mushrooms Gordon is consumed by – they attach and root within, showing us how to forage our way through the shit and harvest joy. Make no mistake, *Fungal* will grow on you in ways you can't imagine."
– Adrienne Gruber, author of *Monsters, Martyrs, and Marionettes: Essays on Motherhood*

Fungal

OTHER TITLES BY ARIEL GORDON

Nonfiction
GUSH: *Menstrual Manifestos for Our Times* (co-edited with Tanis
   MacDonald & Rosanna Deerchild)
Treed: Walking in Canada's Urban Forests

Poetry
Hump
Siteseeing: Writing nature & climate across the prairies
   (co-written with Brenda Schmidt)
Stowaways
TreeTalk

Fungal

Foraging in the Urban Forest

Ariel Gordon

WOLSAK
& WYNN

© Ariel Gordon, 2024

No part of this publication may be reproduced, stored in a retrieval system or transmitted, in any form or by any means, without the prior written consent of the publisher or a license from the Canadian Copyright Licensing Agency (Access Copyright). For an Access Copyright license, visit www.accesscopyright.ca or call toll free to 1-800-893-5777.

Published by Wolsak and Wynn Publishers
280 James Street North
Hamilton, ON L8R2L3
www.wolsakandwynn.ca

Editor: Noelle Allen | Copy editor: Jennifer Hale
Cover and interior design: Marijke Friesen
Author photograph: Mike Deal
Typeset in Minion Pro
Printed by Brant Service Press Ltd., Brantford, Canada

10 9 8 7 6 5 4 3 2 1

The publisher gratefully acknowledges the support of the Canada Council for the Arts and the Ontario Arts Council. We also acknowledge the financial support of the Government of Canada through the Canada Book Fund and the Government of Ontario through the Ontario Book Publishing Tax Credit and Ontario Creates.

Library and Archives Canada Cataloguing in Publication

Title: Fungal : foraging in the urban forest / Ariel Gordon.
Names: Gordon, Ariel, 1973- author.
Identifiers: Canadiana 20240361865 | ISBN 9781989496923 (softcover)
Subjects: LCSH: Mushrooms—Canada. | LCSH: Urban plants—Canada. | LCGFT: Essays.
Classification: LCC PS8613.O725 F86 2024 | DDC C814/.6—dc23

Contents

To Mike and Anna. My favourites!

Mushroom Tourist

FOR THE LAST twenty years, I have mushroom-travelled. Which is not to say that I went on magic mushroom trips. No, just that whenever I travelled, I would go for walks – solo ones I researched in advance and ones with friends to their favourite walking spots – and while walking, I would look for mushrooms.

Some people use travel as a way of broadening their horizons; I use it as a way to add more mushrooms to my repertoire. It's become my way of being in the wider world: when in doubt, walk under the trees and look for mushrooms.

And then take pictures of those mushrooms and post them to social media, because I want people to feel some of the same connection I feel in those moments. The same pleasure.

During the three-plus years of the Covid-19 pandemic, it became harder to travel as widely as we were all used to. The concurrent climate crisis, as evidenced by grinding drought, wildfire smoke and stunted crops, also made me reconsider how much and how often I wanted to travel once things got back to some kind of normal.

So I tried to sightsee in my home place – my yard, my neighbourhood and my city – while also travelling within the prairie provinces between variant outbreaks.

This is my mushroom diary from these years, though really it is more like a bundle of picture postcards from me to the world. Or a stack of flash cards where the test I'm cramming for is surviving the world.

March 28, 2021

Went for a willowy walk in Assiniboine Forest today, where I also found a pre-bent hoop of dogwood whose red-orange almost matched the orange-red of my long sweater-coat, an enormous conk – a shelf-like bracket-shaped fruiting body of certain fungi that grow on trees, that are hard like trees – and some other small mushrooms nearby . . .

[The splitgill mushroom or *Schizophyllum commune* is small and grey-white and furred. It is the mushroom you would expect the White Witch to be wearing as decoration on her person/robes/carriage in Narnia. I found it clustered along the entire length of a young trembling aspen.]

April 11, 2021

I found a mushroom that has it all, including a moustache of pixie-cup lichens and moss. It was the only mushroom I was able to get close to, as it was right next to the boardwalk at the Brokenhead Wetland Interpretive Trail. (This was my first time there, though I'd heard about it for years!) There were various lichens and mushrooms everywhere in the white cedar swamp as well as red carnivorous pitcher plants glittering in the sun but I very carefully stayed on the boardwalk. I was grateful to have the opportunity to walk in this place, that it was made available to me. Some of the time I lay down on the boardwalk so I could see mushrooms better, but that's as close as I got . . .

[A polypore, which is a mushroom with pores for dispersing spores instead of gills, with bands of green and brown and cream, with silvery-green lichen and forest-green moss blurring the distinction between mushroom and tree. You can see the dark soil here, how it is crossed with brown conifer needles.]

April 25, 2021
My partner Mike and I took our AstraZeneca vaccine hangovers to Little Mountain Park, looking for late prairie crocuses. In the whole park, we only found three, and only when we remembered to look in the same spot as last year. Their translucent lilac is what gets me, I think, inflates me like a hot-air balloon, but it should go without saying that I am always on the lookout for mushrooms. When it's unseasonable, my best bet is always the more durable mushrooms that grow on wood instead of from the soil.

[A stack of creamy mushrooms on a downed log, like a plate full of pancakes plunked down in front of you.]

May 24, 2021
We drove out to the Belair Provincial Forest yesterday to look for morels. Found a bunch of false morels (*Gyromitra* spp.), abandoned cars, tiny wild strawberries, emerging bracken, new-to-me wildflowers and six drive-home ticks instead.

[*Gyromitra* is also known as brain fungus, which goes a long way to explaining what this palmful of gorgeous deep-brown mushroom looks like. Also: experimental chandelier/airship.]

May 29, 2021

Mike and I finally found morels, likely *Morchella americana*! At Belair! But only a squat handful after two to three hours of wandering, the woods a new-to-me mix of conifers and trembling aspen. Still, it was very nice to go out looking for morels and then to find morels. (Mike spotted them first, the bastard . . .)

[Imagine three mushrooms with brown-black honeycombed heads and stems that are simultaneously beige and taupe. Dust them with soil and sand and you're there.]

June 19, 2021

Drove out to the Brokenhead Wetland Interpretive Trail again to ogle orchids, pitcher plant flowers and mushrooms. I had never seen so many wild orchids, from the big showy pink and white ones to tiny subtle ones you'd hardly notice if you weren't looking for them. White cedar swamps are new-to-me and sooooo cool. By which I mean interesting but also having a mineral feeling that oak/aspen parkland lacks.

[A pale brown polypore on a cut log on the ground, which holds a diversity of new green and a browned cedar frond . . .]

July 20, 2021

I found a mushroom on a stump along Wolseley Avenue near my house. It doesn't look like much but it's been so dry that I haven't spied a single mushroom all summer so I thought I'd better take/

post a pic to remind myself that they exist. (I exaggerate but not by much, given how yellow/dead the surrounding grass was.)

[A cluster of past-their-due-date oyster mushrooms – usually a choice edible – on a broad grey stump just inside someone's property line. The edges of some caps split, others withered.]

August 29, 2021

Two tiny lawn-shrooms, picked and placed on the stump of my mother-in-law's rosy pink crabapple. She was surprised that I wanted the apples but settlers have been making cider from Manitoba's native crabapples for generations. I made applesauce from its fruit for ten years, boiling them whole and straining out the cores. At first, I dumped everything in a colander and used a spatula to extrude the applesauce but I asked for, and got, a food mill for Xmas, from my mother-in-law, I think!

I am not very interested in Christmas, which is to say the birth of Jesus Christ, but there's no escaping it in Canada. Carols on the radio, Secret Santa gift exchanges at work, emails from my generous MiL, asking for our wish lists. So I use the word "Xmas," which to me means the secular aspects of the holiday.

All of which is to say: I have picked crabapples from this tree's lower branches, bent so low with fruit so that I could put out my hand and pick, and branches almost beyond my reach. My daughter, Anna, was always so drawn to the ladder, those times I dragged it under the tree, to get me and my hungry hands higher.

[Two tiny mushrooms, one white and one yellow, their gills impossible but also sort of like birds' wings, lying on a weathered grey background.]

September 13, 2021

I find a bustling mushroom metropolis. I am staying at St. Peter's Abbey in Muenster, Saskatchewan, working on a poetry manuscript and we have decided to go for a walk en masse. A gaggle of poets, looking at shaggy manes popping up on the lawn and elm oyster mushrooms growing from the cut edges on trees, at the abbey's gloriously productive gardens – flowers and vegetables, shrubs and herbs – and its aging trees. We listen to the sheep bleating from a distant pasture and geese honking from the pond, to our soft exclamations at finding ourselves here, swamped by fall sun. While the others exclaim over the abbey's honey house, I find a mushroom in the understory. It is past its prime, but then, so am I.

[The underside of a pale mushroom with grey-and-brown gills, in the midday sun, teeming with small pale insects, travelling up and down and through the gills.]

September 19, 2021

A *Leccinum* mushroom, with its polypore cap and scabrous stalk, from today's walk in Assiniboine Forest. They are suddenly enormous and everywhere, which is my favourite mushroom trick.

[I stood the bolete up on my hand, like a magic trick, to reveal the creamy white pores of the cap and the bulbous cream/black stem.]

September 23, 2021

Another day, another mushroom, this one an elm oyster or *Hypsizygus ulmarius* on a tree in Omand's Creek Park, which is the halfway point in my local walk, the Wolseley/Wellington loop. Some people call that route "The Full Rachel" after a runner who lived in Wolseley and loved that run. (Now I want the route I take most often in Assiniboine Forest to be called "Ariel's I-only-have-an-hour"!)

[A gilled mushroom the size of my fist growing from a branch scar on an elm, its stem textured, its gills purest white. I especially like that it looks like itself but also like a marble sculpture.]

October 3, 2021
So I found what *appears* to be a lobster mushroom (*Hypomyces lactifluorum*) but it is really the sun, fallen and rustling in the oak leaves at our feet . . .

[This unusually shaped lobster mushroom – round and flat instead of bent and furled – is mottled with deep reds and pale oranges. It is surrounded by dying grass and the olive of aspen leaves, fading from lemon yellow after falling to the ground.]

December 27, 2021
Winter mushrooming isn't as varied as other times of year but I still look for them when walking in Assiniboine Forest. Polypores are your best bet, or mushrooms that were protected from the elements somehow, either in the shadow of fallen logs or by rocky outcrops. Lichens, which consist of a fungal partner with a bacteria or an algae or both, also make for good mushrooming.

[The deep browns of young aspen brackets or *Phellinus tremulae*, dusted with snow that looks like granulated sugar, on a grey-brown aspen trunk, everything else shades of white.]

January 16, 2022
A greeny conk on a trembling aspen beside the path in Assiniboine Forest. Normally, aspen brackets are nut-brown and velvety to the touch, like a horse's nose, but this one is old. It was a beautiful day in the forest . . .

[What looks like a brittle turtle's shell growing out of a branch scar on a whiter-than-usual trembling aspen, the sky mostly haze.]

April 11, 2022
I was planning to walk the Bunn's Creek Trail today but instead walked *around* the flooded creek, taking residential streets to keep the creek in view. For a second, I mistook an ice and sand mushroom by the side of the road for a real mushroom. But it was only an effect created by an entire winter of sand and a fresh layer of ice, by the great melt. It is a great accomplishment, these days, to walk next to a road and not get splashed by passing cars.

[The entire trail under water, the riverbanks erased by water. No mushrooms anywhere, though everything sodden.]

April 30, 2022
I spent my puddle-walk in Assiniboine Forest today collecting aspen colours/textures and new mushrooms.

[Rows of velvety beige mushrooms on a downed log like lead type being set into a page of newsprint, like a collection of dentures, mostly uppers.]

May 5, 2022
Mushroooooooms! On a burr oak, halfway up the hill from Bunn's Creek.

[Beige-banded polypores on grey-and-brown bark, the ground beneath grey and brown. A long half-drowned spring.]

May 23, 2022
Oh stump-loving wild enoki, a.k.a. velvet foot a.k.a. *Flammulina velutipes*, I love you . . . These mushrooms are one of my only consolations for the loss of our boulevard elms to Dutch elm disease, which is caused by a sac fungi. They are beautiful brown-orange mushrooms and grow in rosettes on leftover elm stumps, like ribbons awarded to prize horses, except they're posthumous awards for trees. Post-humus?

[A sticky bun-sized cluster of mushrooms, growing out of the side of an enormous elm stump, weathered and grey. It might be years before the stump is removed and another tree planted in its place. The house behind the lost tree suddenly without dappled light, without shade.]

May 30, 2022
A misty and then moist Wolseley/Wellington loop this morning, ogling flowering crabapples and boulevard mushrooms. I know mica caps or *Coprinellus micaceus* are ordinary, but I love coming upon a big cluster or even just one or two, like this morning.

[A trio of small brown mushrooms, growing into/around each other in the dew-beaded grass, that have somehow managed to avoid being stomped by the procession of kids walking to school.]

June 25, 2022
Found these gorgeous deep-orange mushrooms, likely cinnabar polypore (*Pycnoporus cinnabarinus*), on a downed trembling aspen in wet Assiniboine Forest. The colour is deepest where it attaches to the log, becoming paler as it moves toward the edge of the cap, which has a white edge. I do so like finding a new-to-me mushroom.

[Stealing language the way this mushroom steals nutrients: sapro-phytic, white-rot decomposer, shelf fungus.]

July 30, 2022

It's chanterelle (*Cantharellus enelensis*) season. It's chicken of the woods (*Laetiporus sulphureus*) and lobster mushroom season. It's oyster mushroom (*Pleurotus* spp.) season. Boletes, even. Today, I was hoping I'd come away with a few mushrooms, but Stephenfield Provincial Park seemed very dry and, also, very manicured. So I saw lots of mushrooms, including this one, but nothing . . . special or, more precisely, edible. Luckily, I'm happy with any mushroom any time and there were lots of wildflowers. I even stood under a Saskatoon and picked warm fruit directly into my mouth.

[An orange mushroom whose cap and gills resemble the skirts and petticoats of a cancan dancer, amongst sun-shot blades of brown-and-green grass.]

August 1, 2022

Aesthetically, I inhabit the midsummer space between weathered elm stumps and clumps of mica caps, surrounded by greenery. I want to somehow insert myself, like a bookmark marking a favou-rite passage.

[A grey and weathered stump, whose stark lines are softened by the feathery compound leaves and yellow flowers of silverweed and a newly emerged cluster of caramel-coloured mushrooms.]

August 31, 2022

After two weeks in southern Ontario, the last walk we did was the Mill Race Trail in St. Jacobs. A mushroom was growing in a hol-low in an ash tree and it was the mushroom that made that whole hot walk worth it, especially knowing that emerald ash borer is on its way to decimating every ash tree in Ontario.

[The strangeness of seeing a hollow in a still-standing tree. The wonder of seeing a mushroom with a cap the colour of a deer's hide filling that space.]

September 6, 2022

I scrabbled around the slopes of Bunn's Creek this morning, realizing that much of it was full of broken glass and china. But I also collected mushrooms with my camera, including a pair of beautiful polypores, only realizing afterward that I'd photographed the same ones from the same angle back in May . . .

[Two brown-banded polypore mushrooms on ridged bark in dappled light, the undergrowth shades of brown and grey and green.]

September 20, 2022

Yesterday, I went and walked around the West End with Julia-Simone Rutgers, a *Free Press* reporter, looking at and talking about trees (and mushrooms and cities and climate change). One of my favourite activities! I showed them the nuts on an Ohio buckeye, newly planted on the boulevard and, as if it was my reward, I found an enormous new-to-me mushroom, the dryad's saddle or *Polyporus squamosus*, encountered on the remains of an elm stump. I gently removed it, wanting to take it home and make a spore print. Of course my bag was full, so I walked six blocks with the mushroom in my hand.

[A brown-and-gold dinner-plate-sized mushroom with flattened scales, shadowing both the dried grey wood of an elm stump and prickly weeds next to the stump.]

September 24, 2022
My best thing about today's walk at the Weston Family Tall Grass
Prairie Interpretive Centre, besides hearing Sarah Ens's poems?
Finding a burr oak with three types of lichen on it: green, grey and
orange. The second-best thing? Getting homemade donuts from
an Amish man at the farmers' market in Vita, MB, the community
just past the turnoff for the interpretive centre.

[A side-plate-sized clump of green lichen on ridged brown-and-
grey bark, the browning tall grass behind it.]

September 25, 2022
There's a spot across the street from my house, in a dip below a
youngish boulevard tree, that is always producing mushrooms. I
will often be sitting on my steps and see someone stop and notice
the clusters, which makes me happy, as a mushroom tourist of long
standing. Today I was heading somewhere on foot but stopped to
look at not one but two clusters of mushrooms that were new-
to-me instead of the usual velvet foots or mica/inky caps, which
I still can't quite tell apart. The reason we get so many boulevard
mushrooms is, of course, because there is so much deadwood
underground left over from a century of urban tree-planting.
Sometimes, I could swear there is more deadwood than live,
despite our three million trees.

But it is also true that boulevard mushrooms are the best and
most accessible mushrooms.

[A cluster of grey mushrooms on the grass, amidst clover. Looking
like a heap of stones, a geologic wonder, like a harvest of some
heirloom potato.]

October 24, 2022

I spotted a big clump of velvet foot on an elm stump this morning while walking the Wolseley/Wellington loop. I'm hoping we'll get another good week or so of mushrooms, what with this morning's rain . . .

[A colony of reddy-brown mushrooms against a grey background, with blades of green grass here and there. They look like a toothsome tear-and-share, like a tray of cinnamon buns that have overgrown their pan, but also like a fairy godmother's stash of teeth. Have you ever seen the orange teeth of a porcupine, high up in a tree?]

December 27, 2022

Dragged myself out of the house, coughing, for a walk in Assiniboine Forest with Jordi Malasiuk, a childhood friend. She had a glorious new made-in-Ukraine sweater-coat. I found a wasp's nest, which resembles nothing so much as a wad of grey-and-white paper. So we were roughly even, yes? Also, I spied some aspen brackets in the trees and waded through the snow so I could take a picture. I had a burst of energy post-walk, which I promptly spent grocery shopping.

[A stack of polypore mushrooms on the grey-and-white bark of a trembling aspen. There is what looks like sawdust on the tops of the mushrooms.]

January 5, 2023

Went for a glorious walk in Assiniboine Forest this afternoon with writer friend Samantha Beiko, the sun on little bits of frost in the branches. We have pledged to walk at least once a month, so I can see her and air all my complaints about the writing life like laundry but also fill myself up with mushrooms and sky.

[In the foreground is a section of tree trunk, covered in grey bark, then grey-green lichen, then a stack of polypore mushrooms. The sky in the background a pale and earnest blue.]

Mushrooming

MY PARTNER AND I were together for seven years full of walks and hikes, mushrooms and trees, road trips and waxed cups of strong tea – before we got knocked up.

It took us another decade to acquire an additional dependent.

In those ten years – the age of many of my friends' marriages before they busted up – we had a tank full of fish that included Downie, a black Asian upside-down catfish.

We hand-fed Downie shrimp pellets, until those weren't enough and s/he started eating everyone else. (One fish leapt to his/her death to avoid Downie's jaws of death. S/he became fish-jerky between the dresser where the tank sat and the wall. "It smells in my room," my daughter noted.)

We surrendered Downie to the pet store. We didn't mention s/he was a cannibal.

Next we got black-and-white mollies, which are starter fish like tetras, the difference being that they are prolific breeders. One female came preloaded with enough sperm that she gave birth every month for six months. She was the alpha: she got huge and monstrous and wouldn't let any of the other mollies eat, nipping their fins and head-butting them. And then she'd release a brood of baby mollies, which looked like flecks of ash. They'd hide in the aquatic plants we grew in the tank, which came from the store infested with snails. And the starved cousins and sisters of the alpha molly would finally get to eat.

We surrendered entire litters of small black mollies to the pet store.

AFTER WE DRAINED the fish tank, my daughter pined, though she'd shown very little interest in the fish.

"I want a *real* pet," Anna said. "Can we get a real pet?"

The summer after we drained the tank, we found a greeny-yellowy wild salamander swimming in the pool with us at the water park in Portage la Prairie. That fall, someone brought a car-sick hedgehog to daycare. ("It pooped on two of my friends," my daughter reported, excited.)

So we had serious conversations about salamanders, lizards and geckos and then hedgehogs, guinea pigs and rats. Anna pushed for a cat or a dog, though what she really wanted was a perpetual kitten or puppy. I resisted, citing my furry-animal allergies, but was glad that the conversation was about having-a-pet and not about having-a-sister/brother.

Now, I don't watch kitten videos or hunt baby animals on the Internet. But when summer rolled around again and a friend posted pictures of a small white kitten stretched out, yawning, I felt a pang.

A friend of hers was trying to find homes for three kittens, including the white one. It turned out that I knew the friend of a friend, so one Sunday, we went to go see them. The girl could barely contain herself on the way there, but neither of us connected with the kitten, so next we visited a no-kill shelter. I sneezed, my nose dripped, but we were both suddenly determined.

A week or so later, we brought home a half-grown black-and-white cat.

MY BOSS AND I commuted to work together. When I told David Carr we'd gotten a cat, he had one question: "Who's home the most?"

"I am," I answered.

"She'll love you best, then," he said. David noted with pets it's a combination of who spends the most time with them and who feeds them.

This logic could equally be applied to children, of course. Mothers are still most often the ones home with their children when they are babies, primarily because they gave birth to them and have the boobs with which to feed them. But I'm sure half the reason that mothers often have such strong bonds with their children is because they spend all those endless early days and weeks and months with them, skin on skin.

My boss was right. Given a choice, Kitty prefers to sit on my boobs, wedge her knobby spine under my chin and listen to my heartbeat. She bunts my glasses aside, spreading contentment pheromones all over the bones of my face. If she's feeling particularly tender, she licks my eyelids.

According to the Internet, this is submissive behaviour. She also rolls on the ground the moment the front door opens, showing her belly, as if to say, "Hello, big hairless cats! Please love/feed me . . ."

Nowadays, people refer to their pets as furbabies and to themselves as their pets' parents. But I prefer to think of myself as a big
hairless cat that is slightly higher than Kitty in the social hierarchy.
I have certain responsibilities to her – and affection for her – but
I am not her parent.

Last night, after the girl had gone to bed, I was sitting on the
couch and Kitty assumed her usual position. Except this time, she
reached out and softly put her black-and-white paw on my eyelid.
After a few moments, she tucked both paws under her body and
promptly fell asleep.

When I was breastfeeding my daughter, I was often aware that
I was putting my nipple into a mouth full of irrational teeth, that I
was trusting her not to bite me. Kitty's paw is full of sickle-shaped
claws. Her mouth is full of needles. But like with Anna, I am still
willing to offer her my softest bits.

I'm good with animals, even if I don't need them, if that makes
any sense. When I was a tween, delivering newspapers in my neighbourhood, I came to an understanding with each of the neighbourhood dogs. They would stop barking at me when I entered their
territory; some of them would even offer me their bellies to rub.

I was walking down my street one night and saw a dog-shaped
animal twenty feet away. When I got a bit closer, I realized that
it was a red fox. But I still bent down and offered my hand and
said soft things, trying to tempt it to come closer. We looked at
each other for long moments, but it was wild and eventually loped
away. I hold that memory close, the same way I hold the memory
of being twelve years old and watching my late uncle dandle the
impossibly fragile bundle that was my youngest cousin, only two
weeks old, the way I hold the memory of that hot summer when
my daughter was born, how naked we both were.

My daughter had hoped that the cat we rescued would be hers, that it would love her best, but I tell her that Kitty loves all of us differently. I tell her she has to be more patient with the cat, let it come to her, but she's almost ten now and isn't very patient.

What's more, Anna's starting to push me, alternating pouting with correcting every single thing I say. ("You are embarrassing," my daughter insists. I tell her I could be *much* more embarrassing, given half a chance. She squints at me, deciding whether to believe me.)

WE HADN'T PLANNED to have children, but we were glad Anna arrived once she was here. We found ourselves, individually and as a couple, enriched. Deepened.

But that was it: three weeks after her birth, we agreed that we didn't want to have any more children.

Similarly, we only wanted one cat. Not two or three, or a cat and a dog. One cat.

Unlike the elaborate naming ritual with our daughter – whose grandmothers, whose last name – we just called the new cat Kitty, because that's what we'd likely call her anyway. It wasn't quite naming her "Cat," as some people do, but I was amused by how lazy we were.

For the first few years, unlike my daughter, we managed to keep Kitty out of our bed.

But then Kitty started to sleep all day. She didn't want to play with toys or do much of anything, really. It was my first time living with someone with depression. So more cat-based research. The Internet informed me that you should really adopt two bonded cats at once, just so they keep each other company.

Back we went to the no-kill shelter, lured this time by a photo of three female kittens, whose fur was a gorgeous checkerboard of cinnamon and black. Everyone wanted them, but those sisters were bonded and the shelter wanted them to be adopted together. "But their brother is available," the volunteer at the shelter said. She gestured toward a black-and-white kitten, whose fur looked like it would be long like Kitty's.

I liked the symmetry of having two black-and-white cats. Anna liked that he was a kitten, that she had to coax him out of his hiding place in the kitten room.

I THINK PHILIP was ruined because he had too many names.

"Philip Michael Lester," Anna intoned. "The name of my favourite YouTuber."

So Philip it was. Or Fillip. Or Filipino.

Philip was a vocal cat, shouting at us whenever he didn't get what he wanted.

Philip bolted his food every meal and would have bolted Kitty's food if we didn't actively work to prevent that. He would gnaw on anything left out, from loaves of bread to monster zucchini. He also liked to chew on computer cables, strings on mittens, even the elastic on masks. He was curious about water, dumping glassfuls onto laptops. He even started gnawing on plastic clamshells, I think for the texture.

Philip grew fast, turning from a tiny kitten into a bruiser who looked more like a kangaroo than a cat. We were waiting to neuter him until he was six months old, as per the shelter's recommendation, but he was precocious. He started practise-humping Kitty at five months.

She would just *look* at us, pinned under his bulk, accusatory but also resigned. *Can't you DO anything about this,* her expression asked.

So off to the vet he went, screaming from the carrier in the back seat the whole way.

The vet's office called us to pick him up early, after he screamed at them from his cage all day post-procedure and rubbed off all the skin on his nose on its bars.

It wasn't all bad. He was a great weight-loss program for Kitty, chasing her all over the house, honing her hiding and jumping skills. They sometimes sat next to each other on the couch, alternating licking each other until one or the other of them got mad and left.

The shelter had told us that female cats were usually dominant in these situations, but Kitty just . . . wasn't. It didn't help that he was nearly twice as big as she was. That he was confident and she was timid.

Philip didn't mind Anna carrying him around the house and exclaiming over him at first, but when he was fully grown, he would only allow it for so long before grumbling and taking a swat at her.

Similarly, he sat on all of us on the couch at first, but eventually came to prefer to sit on Mike's legs, with his head resting on the curve of Mike's belly. Given that Kitty wouldn't let him touch her, Mike was very pleased with this new development.

We started calling him Philip-the-Asshole, in real life but also on the Internet. Some people cheered him and his badness. Others said they didn't understand when people said their pets were assholes, that they couldn't be assholes.

It felt the same as when I said my tween daughter was "mostly useless" and people looked at me askance.

"What? She won't do housework, she's bad at housework when forced to do it. She won't even pick berries when there are berries to be picked and I ask nicely."

But his asshole-ness was a good sorting hat: it helped me know who I could be friends with and who I couldn't.

THE WORD "MUSHROOMING" has several meanings.

According to the *Oxford English Dictionary*, it first appeared in 1800 and meant "the gathering of mushrooms." Straightforward, right? Easy.

My favourite usage of the word is from something called *Baily's Mag* in 1867: "The delights of those twin pleasures of autumn, nutting and mushrooming."

Another meaning is "the deformation of something into a mushroom shape; *spec.* the flattening and expansion of a bullet on impact." That definition sadly became common as of 1887.

For this essay, I'm most interested in the third definition – "the very rapid growth or expansion *of* a thing" – whose first usage the *OED* traces to 1916.

In the January issue of the National Fire Protection Association magazine, someone wrote, "Skylights should be glazed with plain thin glass which will readily break when attacked by fire, thus affording a vent, and preventing mushrooming of fire on upper floors."

We'd gone from a couple who couldn't imagine having dependents of any kind to a household with two adults in their forties – who looked something like they looked in their mid-twenties, some family resemblance – one tween and two cats.

We didn't understand how it had happened: the aging, the argumentative child, the cats who couldn't work out who was dominant.

But we went with it. We prevented the mushrooming of fire onto upper floors.

DURING THE PANDEMIC, Anna became depressed and anxious. She might have experienced both without the isolation of lockdown or the long periods where school happened via Zoom, but like a stray cat that stays, like a clump of mushrooms that appears on the boulevard or in a houseplant, it was undeniable.

We managed to find her a great therapist. I tried to mix encouraging her to do the things that were suddenly impossible and not pushing too hard.

One day, in the summer of 2021, she came to us and said she wanted a cat of her own.

"Kitty is yours," she said, looking deep into my eyes, "and Philip is Dad's."

I was about to shout: "*No way! No more cats!*" And then I stopped myself.

For years before we had Anna, I had said that I didn't want to have children. For years before we got Kitty, I was known to say, "We need another dependent like I need a hole in the head." But then things changed. They mushroomed, over years and all at once.

I looked at her, pale and sad, knowing that she'd been rattling around our house like a stone in a shoe. I'd felt the same way for the long months of my maternity leave, but I could see that Anna was growing, that she wouldn't be so terrifyingly dependent on me forever.

But the pandemic was different. None of us – the government, the schools, the doctors, the pundits, the anti-vaxxers – had any way of knowing how long it would last. It had already felt like forever, like a rampaging toddler you hadn't planned for.

Anna was never alone in our house. But she was achingly lonely.

So I stared into Mike's eyes, over her head, and said, "Okay." His face shuffled through a number of expressions, he opened his mouth, then his eyes drifted over to her and he understood.

Anna started haunting the available-cats sections of the websites of animal rescues and no-kill shelters. She developed a short list.

We settled on a two-year-old ginger cat from the Humane Society, via a pet food store in the middle of a hot asphalt parking lot. Because of the pandemic, we had to go in one at a time, with the other two peering through the plate-glass windows, overheating in the parking lot.

From the inside of his enclosure, near a stack of cat food, the cat licked my fingers thoroughly when I was in the store. He licked Anna's and Mike's hands thoroughly when they were in the store.

We pounced.

We named him Twig. Unlike the rescue shelter we'd adopted from before, the Humane Society had no idea of his history.

Like the pandemic, we just had to accept that this was who he was, that this was who we were.

Twig is friendly with all the humans. He is a great snuggler and doesn't mind being carried around like a baby. But he viciously herds the other two cats.

Suddenly, I also had an anxious cat. Kitty was clearly suffering, becoming even *more* timid, so we broke our other long-standing rule: no cats in our bedroom.

At first, Kitty would spend the afternoons there, sleeping in the precise spot on our bed where I lay at night.

When I lay on the bed during the day, reading or avoiding everyone else, she would come press herself up against my leg, purring.

Eventually, she started sleeping overnight in our room. She would appear in the living room around 10:00 or 11:00 p.m., staring at me, until I went upstairs.

"Isn't it time for bed?" her expression asked.

And, after years of sleep deprivation, after going to bed at 1:00 or 2:00 a.m. so I could get everything done, I realized she was right. It *was* time for bed.

WHEN I THINK about our household, the cats and the humans, I flash back to an episode from when we had just one cat.

One day, between karate lessons and groceries, Anna was hungry, so we stopped at Tim Hortons for a bagel with cream cheese. And she pouted because I wouldn't get her a frozen lemonade or a maple cinnamon French toast bagel, restricting her to the tap water I'd brought from home and a twelve-grain bagel.

We'd made it through the drive-through and were sitting at the light and she was lifting my water bottle to her mouth when the light changed. I moved smoothly into the intersection and had just completed my left turn when she yelped.

"What?" I said.

"*Waaaaaah,*" she replied.

"Anna, what?"

"You – jerked – the car . . ."

"Anna, I was driving. I didn't jerk the car."

"You made me spill the water all over myself . . ."

A sniffly moment of silence.

"Here, blot yourself." I passed her the box of tissues I keep in the front of the car.

"I don't even know what that means."

"It means pat yourself with the tissues."

"Like that'll make a difference . . ."

"Anna –"

"What!?!"

"I'm starting to get mad . . ."

We spent the rest of the drive to the grocery store in silence. After we'd found a parking space, I handed the girl a loonie and asked her to go get a cart. I'd opened the trunk and was preparing to transfer our bags and bins to the cart when Anna returned, parking it next to the car.

"Mama," she said, her face pink from crying and bashful. "Can I have a hug?"

And I didn't need the Internet to tell me that this was submissive behaviour or, more simply, that she was looking for reassurance. That she was trying to apologize for shouting at me and for pouting before that. But the difference between Anna and Kitty and even the neighbourhood dogs of my childhood is that my relationship with my daughter is slippery; we are both alternately dominant and submissive, sad and looking for solace. More than that, we are just people, trying to get along, even if I built her in my body, cell by cell, limb by limb.

"Yes," I said. And I pulled her close, holding her tighter than usual. I wanted her to remember that, once, neither of us could remember where she began and I ended. I wanted her to hear my heartbeat, thudding irrationally in my chest.

And I was suddenly glad that we were here, damp and irritable, in this parking lot, that we had all made it this far.

My daughter was born in the hospital; Kitty was born under somebody's stairs. Philip is an asshole. But we love each other, and most of the time, we remember that things change, that we can pull back our claws.

Red River Mushroomer

ONE SUNDAY IN October 2021, I wake up at 8:00 a.m. and look at my phone and go pee and then return to bed and look at my phone until 10:30 a.m. This is my version of sleeping in. Also, because my house is small and my family is always there, if I want to be alone, I often find myself either working at the desk in my bedroom we installed during the work-from-home period of the pandemic or lying on the bed.

When I get up for my shower, I call down the stairs, asking Mike hopefully for a cup of tea.

And Anna yells up, "You can come down and make it yourself!"

"I wasn't talking to you!" I yell back down.

Mike, who has booked the next week off so he can stay home and do nothing, otherwise known as a "staycation," eventually brings me tea. It is more than an hour after I asked for it and a half-hour after I texted him "HELLLLOOOOOOO" but he still brings it and I still thank him. I am determined to drink it before it goes cold this time. And for once, I do. I read Eula Biss's *Having and Being Had*, which is about class and money, about capitalism and artmaking. I like this section, based on a conversation between Biss and a taxi driver, about writing and teaching writing: "Do you think it's wrong, he asks, to make your living something that won't earn your students a living? No, I say. And then I pause over why. The service I'm doing for my students, I tell him, is teaching them how to find value in something that isn't widely valued. And I think it's a gift to give another person permission to do something worthless."

I read and play with the cat. Kitty is allowed in our bedroom sometimes and loves it; she will lie pressed next to my blanketed legs and purr as loudly as the radiators did in the old apartment blocks Mike and I lived in, separately and together, in the years before and after we got together. Today I am teaching her the pleasure of being enveloped in blankets. She doesn't mind sitting on a blanketed lap, but has resisted being covered with blankets, which is the one-true-love of the other cats. I have had a fluffy blanket that has lived on the living room couch for years, since we uploaded a pattern made from a drawing of my daughter's to a merch website. Even though we had created a design and assigned it to a product category, none of the blankets were made. It was a theoretical blanket. In order to afford to have a blanket made, we waited until the vendor had one of their semi-regular discount days. We proudly draped it over my daughter's legs when we next sat down to watch a movie. Anna snuggled up under its fluffiness, a smile on her face, then asked, "When will I be paid for it?" We tried not to laugh.

IN NOVEMBER 2020, when I first joined fellow writer Sally Ito on a mudlark – by which I mean a couple of hours walking the banks of Winnipeg's two main rivers, looking for old glass and china in the water or mired in the clay and mud – I couldn't see anything. My eyes were trained for mushrooms, for nuts and seeds, ferns and lichen.

Sally could scan the muddy banks of the Assiniboine and see bits of glass and pottery in amongst the plastic. So much plastic. Slurpee straws, shredded plastic bags, flossers, tampon applicators. All I could see was mud and tree roots, so I missed everything, but I was still happy to be washed with the golden light, the cold air.

By spring the following year, I was doing a bit better with finding man-made things. But it didn't help that the riverbank, especially on the Assiniboine, was a stark place, mostly river-carved Red River gumbo. Which is to say: everything covered in, blurred by, a layer of mud and clay.

My photographs from a May 2021 mudlark were typical of this era in my mudlarking "career." We had decided to explore the riverbank behind the Granite Curling Club, founded in 1880 and marked by a Tudor-framed clubhouse that now has a heritage designation. As we worked our way down the bank, the gumbo was leather-hard, dried with cracks so that the surface resembled a set of irregular plates, laid out across the upper riverbank. If you stepped on them lightly, they'd support you, but stomp and they'd collapse and you'd find yourself in soft, sticky mud. Which meant your boots would suddenly be twice their weight. There was a family of geese with goslings the colour of the sunshine, nibbling on fresh shoots of grass, paddling in the silty river. There were raccoon footprints in the mud.

I found a modern tart pan in the water, only slightly crushed, which I used to store my finds. I found the base of a fishy sculpture, a stylized fin in black stone or ceramic. I found two highly textured pieces of brown ceramic that looked like feathers, like they'd come from a pigeon-deterring statue of an owl.

But I was most excited to find a clump of dusty mushrooms, the same colour as the mud they'd grown out of, halfway up the bank. They looked like fossils of mushrooms instead of mushrooms, but I was determined to spore print them, to get to know them better. When I got home I realized that they were too old and dry for spore printing, but tried anyway. Instead of spores, I got a fine dusting of dried mud on my paper.

I called them "gumbo mushrooms" on social media, but looking back, they were probably *Agaricus* sp., the button or field mushroom. Yes, the same mushroom that is now cultivated commercially as white or brown or cremini or portobello mushrooms.

What I remember now about that mudlark was how relieved I was to find mushrooms.

My old friends.

training my eye
for blots of colour in a mass
of green – tree & shrub-layer, grass
& sedge & pot-herb – for bone-white & milk-tea,
peel-orange. I can spot a gelatinous blob at twenty paces
but I mistake golf for puff until I'm close enough to tee off. Lu
ckily, I swing both ways: pointing a lens up a mushroom's skirt for
the gills AND sniffing rotting-animal funk from stinkhorn caps. I am
conked & stumped but remember: every mushroom is edible once. N
ever mind wood ticks, hanging from my earlobes & all the times
I plunked myself
down in poison
ivy, itchy bliste
rs raising on my
thighs like mino
r demons before
I got back to the
parking lot. Nev
er mind twigs in
my hair, burrs tu
cked in cuffs & s
oft crevasses: I'm
privy to the pulp
& paper world bre
aking down. Stand
ing over a mushro
om – oyster & lob
ster, coral & morel –
I know we are all mu
lch, building & falling in a week. We're fucked, but
this poem, composed with inky cap sludge, ties me into
a party line, a history of roots & mycelia, suckers & fruiting
bodies: *Helllllllo?*

THE OTHER COUCH blanket, the one I prefer, is Mike's baby blanket, made for him by his paternal grandmother. It was made using a pattern/yarn that is uniquely of the '70s: an ugly white/green/neon yellow in a large chevron pattern. I have used it now longer than he did, back when he was a baby. I have spent years with it blurring the outline of my legs.

Up in our room, I'd pulled the fluffy blanket out of a basket of clean laundry when I'd had the flu a few weeks ago, when I was fully dressed and achy, when I didn't want to get into bed but wanted to lie on the bed and rest. So I draped the blanket over me and it was just enough to be cozy. It had lived on the end of the bed or on the chair next to the bed since. Yesterday, I covered Kitty with it and waited to see what would happen. She lay under it for an hour, her outline almost erased by the haphazard shapes the blanket made. Today, I did it again, but we played a game of hide-and-seek, where I would tap on the blanket on top of her and she would try to catch my fingers, kneading the blanket, getting her claws caught in the blanket. She then spent five minutes carefully and delicately licking my fingers, especially my pointer finger and thumb – my phone fingers – with her tulip tongue.

THE THINGS THAT draw my eye on the riverbank – sprigs of flowers or gilt on a sherd of pottery, bits of coloured glass in ornate patterns, fragments of doll heads or figurines – are parts of things that I have absolutely no interest in collecting when not on the riverbank. Which is to say: collecting old china bits hasn't made me more interested in buying sets of china, even if I could find a matching pattern. I hate candy dishes. I never really liked dolls. The mudlarking YouTubers that I watch – because it makes me feel like I'm in good/weird company, because it helps me "get my eye in" – are mother-daughter teams or husband-wife duos. They'll sometimes collect beer or soda bottles but they're most excited by the small. Buttons, marbles, vials and glass bottle stoppers, anything small or cute, are among their favourite finds.

I collect along various lines on the riverbank, but I am as drawn to the big chunks of waste glass as I am to the teacup handles.

Once, when Sally found a marble and was exclaiming about it, I muttered, "If you liked finding one, I could go to a dollar store and get you a whole bag for a coupla bucks. I'd seed the riverbank with them."

She laughed. It was true, marbles were common and cheap, even as recently as my childhood, and aren't worth much as antiques, unless they're really old. But we both knew I was *also* a bit jealous, not having found a marble of my own to that point.

But finding something cool on the riverbank has nothing to do with value, really. The bits and pieces we find are souvenirs of the two or three hours we spend on the riverbank, in ourselves.

Similarly, I've gone mushrooming with people who are only interested in mushrooms if they can eat them. I like mushrooms in the context of the ecosystem they grow in and I like them because of how varied, how ugly and beautiful they are. I was hurt and confused by these people's disinterest in mushrooms-as-mushrooms, in mushroom-hunting as part of the experience of walking in the woods.

More recently, working in a mushroom factory where no one talked about how lovely the mushrooms were – in fact, people commented about how they'd stopped eating mushrooms as a result of working with them, that their cultures didn't have much of a history of eating mushrooms – made me see mushrooms, temporarily at least, as commodities.

But shards of glass pulled from the river? They can't possibly be assigned a value. They're man-made but still feel natural, somehow. They're wild, tangled in gnawed beaver sticks and enrobed in

Red River gumbo, haphazardly crazed or broken or whole. It's not even clear if the glass, most of it seventy-five or a hundred years old, could be added to the recycling stream.

"What will you *do* with all the things you collect?" I'm often asked by people on my social media feeds, when they're not commentating on how fascinated they are by all the amazing stuff I find, or sliding into my DMs to ask if they can come with me the next time I go out.

They might as well be asking, "What will you *do* with your writing?" Because most of what I write isn't worth anything either: it has low cultural value and is probably the laziest thing a good capitalist would do. I write poetry because I can afford to, though just barely.

Frances Koncan, an Anishinaabe/Slovene playwright who lives in Winnipeg, wrote recently on social media that she's always surprised that her theatre/playwriting peers can afford their careers, until she sees pictures of them at their parents' houses at the holidays and she gets it. They've got the privilege of being from middle- or upper-middle-class families: *of course* they were going to university and *of course* their parents were paying their tuition. Most of them didn't have to have jobs while they were at uni. Most of them lived at home or had their parents pay for their apartments, before and after graduation. And now, if they fail utterly or get sick or just become artists their parents would step in and help, though it's hard to know how long that affluent assistance would be available to them.

I'm too old for these sorts of upper-middle-class signs to show up in my photos, but if I had been taking those sorts of photos twenty or thirty years ago, the results would have been mixed. For instance, when I was growing up my parents had a cabin in Minaki and two cars. But the cabin, while charming and homey, had no electricity or running water and we shared it with my dad's brother's family, and my parents drove their cars until they died.

We also had lots of paying-the-mortgage-aggressively angst, and it was understood that my mother wasn't to buy *extra* things. (She once asked me to not tell Dad when she got me a sweatshirt/pants set on sale . . . and he asked me if it was new the first time I wore it. I lied and said I'd had it for a while, though we both knew it was new.) Of course, all that scrimping was for nothing, because my mother had to remortgage the house when she and my father divorced so she could give him half the value.

(After the cabin was sold, it was torn down to put up a McMansion Summer Home with one wall entirely made of windows.)

WHILE I WAS playing hide-and-seek with Kitty I discovered that she likes to be under the blanket but also to have my face under there with her. When I looked under she started wriggling forward with obvious pleasure to let me scratch her face and underchin. This went on for almost an hour, me in my towel, trying to read my book but mostly sticking my head under the blanket and cooing at the cat. Eventually, I put on underwear, a sports bra and a set of flannel pajamas, because the towel kept shifting as I turned. Kitty took this to be a sign of the end and waited near the closed door to be let out, into the wider world of other cats who chase her off the warm snooze-spot she makes on one end of the couch.

I turned on the overhead light and read some more Eula Biss: "I don't believe you think what you do is worthless, my sister says. I don't. I just mean financially worthless. Writing poetry doesn't usually produce money, for most people. Free verse is doubly free, in that it is unfettered by meter and it has no market value."

I finish my still-warm tea. When Mike had come up to deliver it, I'd made puppy-dog eyes at him, saying, "Hey vacation-man, can you make meeeeee breakfast in bed?" He'd said there isn't much to make, but I mentioned the eggs and bread I knew we had and also the package of uncooked bacon hiding in the meat drawer. But another hour has passed and I'm starting to get super hungry. Hunger headachy. I feel empty but also warm and I find myself falling asleep under the overhead light and the additional light of my bedside lamp even though I'm not tired. I had planned to wait Mike out, to stay in bed until breakfast appeared, but now I'm resigned to going down and getting my own goddamn breakfast. When I get downstairs, Mike is frying bacon and toasting whole wheat bread in the fat. He's also making over-hard eggs, or will once the bacon is finished, also in the fat. I find bacon-fried bread way too decadent most of the time, but he loves it and this time I ask for a piece to honour the slow, lazy morning I've had.

I am sometimes anxious about being productive, but sometimes, reader, you have to invest in utter wastes of time.

I'VE NOTICED THAT a lot of people who have side hustles, making macramé or pottery or small batches of fancy handmade pasta or big bright/ugly dresses, are mostly selling these items to people who look like them. Who maybe also have side hustles or are just happy to spend ridiculous amounts of money on their friend's wares.

"It's like they're just making things to sell to each other," literary organizer/film aficionado/weirdo John Toews noted on our weekly walk out of hippy-dippy Wolseley and along affluent Wellington Crescent and back. He said he didn't understand how they could afford to make or even buy those objects and then, like Frances, he looked more closely, reading all the class markers in the background of photos, in the clothes they were wearing and the restaurants they were selfie-ing in.

My social media is a terrible flirt, in that I make almost no money but take photos at farmers' markets, where I pick up my

CSA veg and buy gum-busting loaves of bread from artisanal bakers. Given my partner's reasonably paid job and my ruinous vocations, we can afford bits and pieces of that life, but I'm a scavenger at heart. I like good food but I also like things cheap or free, bartered or borrowed. I spent two growing seasons trading poems for food, which was nonsense but also enormously satisfying.

My mother asks me sometimes if I'm writing a novel. I started my writing "career" in my early teens with a fantasy novel and I wrote a historical novel for a while in my twenties, but now I mostly write poetry and weird nonfiction. She still wants me to make money off my writing, to show that I've been the slightest bit practical. But I resist her. I know plenty of novelists that don't make any money either and I want to write things about things I love in the genres that seem to fit them best, money be damned.

So when people ask me what I'm going to *do* with my mudlarking finds, I want to say, "Are you asking if mudlarking, if the production and sale of mudlarking crafts, could be my side hustle? As a writer with a day job, I already have a side hustle and a front hustle, thank you kindly. I am hobbled with hustle."

WHEN I'VE GOT toast and bacon but am still waiting for my eggs, I glue together the final two pieces of a broken drugstore bottle I found on the riverbank last week. I found them close to each other, so it was clear they'd fit together, but it was still very satisfying to put them together in my hands and in my brain. They were both covered with a cheap wig of recent zebra mussel byssal threads and a hundred years of caked-on grime. The shards of embossed glass, with their square bottom and round screw-top, swam first in a bath of denture cleaner for the grime and then in diluted bleach for the byssal threads. This process took days – a couple of days in one soak, then another couple in the other. I've been gluing them together in stages, first a small fragment glued onto a larger one, and then the Frankensteined big pieces together.

It is like magic, seeing broken things fit together to make some kind of whole.

Mudlarking is an exercise in brokenness, in being satisfied with brokenness, in our wonky humanity. It's a reminder that we can make lovely things that will persist, but that they can't and won't remain intact. That can be a china plate that becomes a china sherd or a plastic toy from China that becomes microplastics. These things can be benign or malignant.

Mushrooming is about remembering the loveliness of the natural world. It is about ephemerality: the mushrooms you find today, glorying in their shape and texture, will not be there in a week's time. Mushrooms vanish but add to the soil where they decay, they break down dead trees and provide food for other organisms, unlike glass and ceramic.

While I shake my head at my settler ancestors, their friends and colleagues, who saw a beautiful river and thought, "Now here's a good place to stow this garbage," I see mushrooms as a different kind of magic, one that the natural world makes just for me. The variety of shapes, sizes and textures makes me ache the same way a big box of just-opened crayons makes me ache. It's the easiest way I know to knit up a sweater of happiness.

I'VE BEEN MUSHROOMING for more than twenty years now. Which means that I'm very familiar with mushrooms in Assiniboine Forest's oak aspen forest, with mushrooms on the boulevard in downtown Winnipeg. I'm not an expert, but I'm familiar with the mushrooms that appear every year, most years and some years.

I'm happy to see every mushroom but I only stop to look at and photograph mushrooms that are different, special or weird.

I've been mudlarking for almost two years, which means that I'm still *so* pleased with almost every object that appears in the mud or on top of the mud.

I love being on the riverbank – rooting around like a wild pig eating acorns, like a domesticated pig unearthing truffles – and I love looking forward to being there again.

I CAN'T STOP thinking about the flotillas of geese and ducks, the floating islands of beavers. The eagle that hunts the river corridor. The rowing shells and motorboats that glide and growl. The people who live under the bridge and in the strip of woods between the river and the walking path. The serious cyclists and the ice-cream strollers on the path and the squealing bridge beyond.

I can't stop thinking about the clumps of volunteer tomato plants we found, ripening in several spots on the bank, how I put the tomatoes I picked in the only not-muddy pocket of my mud-larking bag. How I felt leery about eating them unwashed from the riverbank and then eating them at all, given the pollution, the dumped metals and plastics, and the semi-occasional eruptions of sewage into the river.

When I got home I piled them in my countertop tomato thingy and then two friends gave me tomatoes from their gardens, which I piled on top, and then a day or so later I realized I couldn't remember which was which and I just ate them like they were food and not symbolic objects.

Besides finding hundred-year-old objects on the riverbank in the middle of the city, I think I like getting dirty best of all. It makes me feel wild and woolly. It makes me feel excited and calm. I'm sorting not just china and glass but what it means to live in a city, all the strange histories we dump in the river.

IT WAS NOVEMBER 2022 and I was walking with historian and troublemaker Adele Perry toward the Burton Cummings Theatre to see singer-songwriter William Prince perform, when she mentioned that she had been rereading the text of the Selkirk Treaty, as one does.

The treaty was signed at what we now know as the Forks on July 18, 1817. That's a hundred years older than most of the glass and china on my stretch of the riverbank, which is within walking distance of the Forks.

Adele told me that she found something in the text of the treaty that I might find interesting and said she'd send it to me the next day.

Witnesseth that for and in consideration of the annual present or quit rent hereinafter mentioned, the said Chiefs have given, granted and confirmed, and do, by these presents, give, grant and confirm unto our Sovereign Lord the King all that tract of land adjacent to Red River and Ossiniboyne River, beginning at the mouth of Red River and extending along same as far as Great Forks at the mouth of Red Lake River, and along Ossiniboyne River, otherwise called Riviere des Champignons, and extending to the distance of six miles from Fort Douglas on every side, and likewise from Fort Daer, and also from the Great Forks and in other parts extending in breadth to the distance of two English statute miles back from the banks of the said rivers, on each side, together with all the appurtenances whatsoever of the said tract of land, to have and to hold forever the said tract of land and appurtenances to the use of the said Earl of Selkirk, and of the settlers being established thereon, with the consent and permission of our Sovereign Lord the King, or of the said Earl of Selkirk. Provided always, and these presents are under the express condition that the said Earl, his heirs and successors, or their agents, shall annually pay to the Chiefs and warriors and successors, or their agents, shall annually pay to the Chiefs and warriors of the Chippeway or Saulteaux Nation, the present or quit rent consisting of one hundred pounds weight of good and' merchantable tobacco, to be delivered on or before the tenth day of October at the forks of Ossiniboyne River – and to the Chiefs and warriors of the Killistine or Cree Nation, a like present or quit rent of one hundred pounds of tobacco, to be delivered to them on or before the said tenth day of October, at Portage de la Prairie, on the banks of Ossiniboyne River. Provided always that the traders hitherto established upon any part of the above-mentioned tract of land shall not be molested in the possession of the lands which they have already cultivated and improved, till His Majesty's pleasure shall be known.

Adele thought I'd enjoy that the Ossiniboyne, now known as the Assiniboine, was once also known as Rivière des Champignons, which translates to "River of Mushrooms." And I liked that very much, but it reminded me that sometimes I forget that the river was named for the Assiniboine people, that the land around the river was the territory of the Saulteaux and Cree Nations.

I do some surface research on William Prince and discover that he's Saulteaux and the direct descendent of Chief Peguis, one of the signatories of Selkirk's treaty in 1817.

So we're all connected in settler colonialism, in ideas of value, whether we like it or not.

My own piece of settler colonialism was sold in 2001 for $103,000, in 2004 for $135,000 and in 2009 for $242,000. In eight years, the house increased in value by two and a half times. How is that possible? That last price, the one we paid, comes in under the average Manitoba house price in April 2020, which was $295,000, though I should note that our house would probably sell for close to that now. It comes in far below the 2020 average for Ontario at $594,000 or British Columbia at $736,000.

Sometimes it's hard to have to remember how many times the land, where I mudlark and where I live, has traded hands in the two hundred years since Selkirk's Treaty and the numbered treaties that followed.

It's hard to know how terribly we've treated the land we paid so little and then so much for.

IN NOVEMBER 2021, I was in the middle of my third week of working at the mushroom factory, my last week on the training crew, and my two days off felt unreal, like they weren't my real life. I was irritable because a part of me wanted to be in a big empty room that was the same temperature as my perimenopausal skin, as my barely contained blood, to be peering at a shelf covered in white mushrooms. Where all I had to do was shuffle down the row and pick mushrooms.

I didn't last long on the real crew I was assigned to because my picking with them was messy: full of shouting people and uncertainty about what or how I should pick. Not meditative, not self-directed, not quiet, like my first three weeks on the training crew.

My friend Tessa says that that's the problem with all piecework. The work itself is fine, even enjoyable, but when you have to speed up to make good money, when you're on a crew that depends on every member to be speedy, that's when the impatience with anything that slows them down and the resultant shouting to *Hurry up!* or *What's the holdup?* begins.

Going mudlarking is less regular than harvesting mushrooms, but it is just as real/unreal. It is all about seeing and recognizing familiar shapes from being a consumer in this culture: bottle-shape, jar-shape. It is about reaching down and touching the odd-shaped things, the remnants of previous generations that we don't use or manufacture any more. Busted machine parts. Broken bricks. Rusted horse tack.

I spent half my time on the riverbank bent over or squatting and the other half scanning the ground around my feet or forward a few feet. It is exactly like mushrooming in that way, how you can walk in one direction, thoroughly searching, and then turn and walk back and see something, or several somethings, that you missed. Sally and I often find things the other has missed on the same small patch of riverbank.

I always find things worth hauling home, hanging them from my body like the weight of years. My bag the same as a baby on my hip, except sharper, clanking. A sink full of dishes. A party's worth of half-drunk bottles, collected on the kitchen counter afterward like a row of participation trophies, each one with a cigarette float-ing in the dregs. Except in this case, raw sewage.

I am always completely taken up. And when I'm finished, feel-ing the pull of home and work, my legs and back sore, my bag full, I am always suddenly famished, thirsty and feeling the urge to pee. And so the walk back to the car is always pleasurably painful.

AFTER YEARS OF excruciating drought, the winter and spring of 2022 were overwhelmingly snowy and then soaking wet. We needed the moisture, but we got So. Much. Moisture.

After training my mudlarking eye at three feet and then six feet in spring 2020 and 2021, the water level in spring 2022 sat at eighteen feet for forty-five days straight, from April to June. That meant that the homeless encampments on the bank were flooded out. That meant the riverbank I knew vanished. Ironically, the places on the bank the unhoused prefer, with dips and valleys that provide some natural shelter, were made from buried garbage. We'd never gotten to investigate these fill hills, because of the encampments, because of the glory of what could be found at the waterline, but now we could.

This debris was later, shifting us into the 1930s and '40s from the 1910s and '20s. In the water-weakened fill hills, I found bottles with early plastic lids, cellulose and Bakelite. I found bottles with bits of labels, bottles that had been printed on instead of embossed. It was a whole new set of things to train my eye on!

I watched the City of Winnipeg's Current River Levels webpage like it was a horoscope. But it did tell me things about my future, because every time the water dropped a foot or a foot and a half, I would go mudlarking, to see what had been exposed, what the receding waters had left for me. And I found more complete bottles than I'd ever found before, including a dozen or more small bottles of the type used by compounding pharmacists. I found toothbrushes with their bristles missing. I found bottle stoppers and 1940s' marbles.

By July 2022, the river water had returned to something approaching normal, sitting between six and seven feet. The ground that had been underwater for most of the growing season, which was now covered in a layer of fertile gumbo, burst into life. What had been a barren muddy expanse, where every curve of the riverbank was exposed, was green Green GREEN.

For Sally and I, mudlarking became more like bushwhacking, except there weren't any paths to step off. One time, crawling over a felled tree, debarked by the river and parked high up the bank by floodwaters, I was thrilled to see coral mushrooms growing along its flank. They're off-white or beige and grow in small clumps and are called coral mushrooms because they look like coral, branching like an elaborate candelabra or pipe organ. The tips of these coral mushrooms look sort of like medieval crowns, with knobs along the circumference, which is why they're called crown-tipped coral (*Artomyces pyxidatus*).

I pointed them out to Sally and pulled out my phone to take a picture.

"Oh wow," she said. "Are they edible?"

"I'm not sure," I said, putting away my phone.

And that's where we left it.

training my fingers
on the jolly bellies, the bell curve of puff
balls, prodding to see the fine mist of spores. The fo
rest floor, all mulch/moss/lichen/ferns & the mushrooms emer
ging, lifting the leaf litter like a car with a flat. Clumps & rosettes
on stumps & rotting logs, single mushrooms on long stems. I flick yel
low puckers of witches' butter, just to see the jelly quiver. Trace the wet
candelabra of coral mushrooms, white teeth of dead man's fingers as they
emerge from the ground, before they wither. *Wait, am I talking about me
or the mushrooms?* My pinky still wonky after falling & then finish
ing the hike, bones snapped like winter-stiff twigs. The
worst part? No more
macho handshakes fo
r me, all squeeze and n
o sizzle. *Oh! It hurts!* The
moist grip of oyster mushroo
ms halfway up a tree is all I can h
andle. But then there's silkiness of b
rown conks on branch scars of tremblin
g aspens. Like horses' noses – I order pe
ople to stroke them. I will kneel to feel und
er the caps of new mushrooms: gills? por
es? You've heard of off-roading, well I
'm an off-path person, my knuckles
studded with mosquito bites, m
ud bas-relief-ing my finge
rprints. Today's tick-count? Three. Scrabbling on the
back of my neck, lower back, chest:
Eeeeeeee!

I PUT ANOTHER piece of bread in the toaster, which I will eat unbuttered, as is my standard operating procedure. My eggs arrive as the toast pops. I pile both pieces, the one sodden with bacon fat and the plain-Jane one, with eggs and bacon, then squirt ketchup on everything. It is glorious and worth the wait, even if I didn't get to eat it in bed.

I don't often take/post pictures of meals, but I felt rich the day I posted a picture of a breakfast in bed Mike had made entirely without prompting.

Similarly, the riverbank is pretty where we go mudlarking. It looks good in pictures. But really, it's like bright red and orange sunsets in smog-shrouded cities: it's polluted. In spots, the bank is made almost entirely of glass. Tonnes of it.

So I don't feel bad about taking away bagfuls: I am a settler garbage man. I am proud of having found a collectible that is literally worthless. Now I have six whole bottles that are a hundred years old. They're worth about the same as a published page of poetry in a literary magazine: ten or twenty or fifty dollars.

Even if I sold all six, it wouldn't pay for even a tenth of the hours I spent looking for them.

Still, I like having a beer bottle that's a hundred years old. They're beautiful objects, the glass clear or aqua or green, the embossing crisp or worn down. I particularly love the bubbles caught in the thick glass, how sometimes one side of the bottles is thicker than the other.

Maybe that's one way of escaping capitalism: to focus all your time on things that no one needs or wants. To have ruinous vocations left and right.

Harvester

IN FOUR WEEKS as a harvester at Loveday Mushroom Farms in the fall of 2021, I picked more than two thousand pounds of mushrooms.

I was harvester 2146. That number was written on the front of my hard hat and printed on the stickers I affixed to every box I filled so I would get paid, this being a piecework-type job. The knife assigned to me, a paring knife with an orange plastic handle, was D46.

And I picked those mushrooms by hand, two or three at a time.

After I'd finished my first week at Loveday – having picked 605 pounds – I was at Food Fare on Maryland Avenue and was browsing their veggie aisle when I came to the mushroom section. "Fresh Manitoba White Mushrooms" the label read, $2.99 per pound. They had two big open boxes of mushrooms and a stack of paper bags with Loveday's logo and slogan – "Growing with

Manitoba Since 1932" – on them, so that people could select the ones they wanted. They also had prepackaged containers.

I had a series of thoughts: "I could have picked these mushrooms!" and "That's a five-pound red!"

I didn't buy any mushrooms that day but I could have told you exactly what size each mushroom was.

LOVEDAY GROWS *AGARICUS bisporus* mushrooms, whose common name is just "mushroom."

The biggest mushroom secret is that white button and brown cremini mushrooms are both varieties of *Agaricus bisporus* and portobello mushrooms are just creminis that have been matured longer before they are picked.

The closest wild equivalent in Manitoba to *Agaricus bisporus* is the field or meadow mushroom (*Agaricus campestris*). Before setting foot in Loveday, I'd collected meadow mushrooms for making spore prints, since mature specimens are easy to find, medium to large in size and full of dark-brown spores. But I'd never eaten them. And while I am happy to see any mushrooms when out on a walk with my camera, I'll often bypass meadow mushrooms in favour of their more brightly coloured or unusually shaped relatives.

But I can see why they were chosen for domestication: they grow prolifically from spring to fall, they're mild in flavour and so adaptable to a variety of cuisines and they're pale white. Nondescript.

ON MY FIRST day, which began with a health and safety video and ended with a tour of the factory, a short white manager named Lisa asked us to not wear heavy perfumes.

"The mushrooms absorb odours," Lisa said. "If I'm standing there and I can smell you, the mushrooms will taste how you smell. Good or bad."

But smells weren't the only things that the mushrooms (and their packaging) could pick up. Besides the usual admonition to not wear open-toed shoes, there were a number of other items on the dress code:

When you come into work, please come in:
- wearing clothing without sequins or gemstones
- with no jewellery
- with no fake eyelashes
- with no fake fingernails
- with no nail polish

One of my favourite memories of that first week was watching Lisa and an Asian supervisor in a hand-embroidered apron carefully, almost tenderly, tape up the sequined hem of a Somali woman's dress. The dress was old and it was one of a few layers that Hawa was wearing, so she'd likely forgotten about the prohibition about sequins or that the dress even had sequins in the first place.

FRED LOVEDAY WAS a bricklayer and recent immigrant from England when he was hired to build Manitoba Mushroom Growers at 27 Marion Street on the banks of the Red River in 1929.

By the time construction was finished, the consortium of owners had gone bankrupt and the courts awarded him the land and building. Loveday convinced his son Bert to leave his job in banking and together they started growing mushrooms. Starting in 1932, MMG sold mushrooms to local restaurants, private clubs, grocers and downtown department stores.

In 1947, the Lovedays purchased a second site, this time on Mission Street in the St. Boniface industrial area. Eventually, all their operations were moved there, a decision that was hastened by the 1950 flood, which damaged the Marion Street location.

By 1953, Bert's son Fred, freshly graduated from the University of Manitoba with a degree in biology, had joined the company. In 1953, MMG started canning mushrooms under the Morning Fresh label. In 1961, the company expanded to Calgary, making the Manitoba Mushroom Growers name obsolete. Loveday Mushroom Farms was born. In 1969, both the canning line and the Calgary farm were phased out.

In 1986, Fred's son Burton, freshly graduated from the University of Winnipeg with a degree in biology, joined the company. In case you're keeping track, the four generations of Lovedays go: Fred, Bert, Fred, Burton.

In 2007, when Loveday released its corporate history, Burton noted that "workers now pick as many mushrooms before 9:00 a.m. every day as did employees of Manitoba Mushroom Growers in an entire year."

By this time, Loveday was selling their mushrooms to the big grocery chains and food distributors in Manitoba, Saskatchewan and northwestern Ontario. Some of the mushrooms are sold under the Loveday name and others under their customers' store brands.

The next expansion was in 2009, to Springfield, Manitoba, thirty minutes outside Winnipeg. At that point, Loveday was producing nearly 73,000 kilograms of mushrooms a week at the two plants. When I started work there a dozen years later, all composting and packaging was done at Mission and all growing and harvesting in Springfield.

In 2020, Burton Loveday sold the company to South Mill Champs, a company based out of Pennsylvania. South Mill Champs had also recently purchased BC's Champ's Mushrooms, a former Loveday competitor. According to Martin Cash's *Winnipeg Free Press* article on the sale, "South Mill has multiple production facilities in Pennsylvania just west of Philadelphia – where about one half of the mushrooms grown in North America come from – and Champs has about eight facilities in B.C."

Martin quotes South Mill CFO Sergio Varela on the benefits of the Loveday acquisition: "We had both coasts covered fairly well with large operations on both coasts. The part that was missing was the middle of the continent. You have to be there to be able to supply within 48 hours to our customers. That was the key strategy for the transaction, the geographic nature of where Winnipeg is."

Despite the ownership change, Loveday Mushroom Farms is still Canada's oldest continuous producer of mushrooms. And when they say continuous, they don't just mean year after year – they mean day after day. While Xmas tree farmers call their product the "last harvest" of the traditional growing season, farmed mushrooms are grown and harvested all year.

"Because they are very perishable, a lot of our customers want seven day a week delivery," Burton Loveday noted in a 2014 interview with CBC. "So we pick, pack and ship mushrooms everyday of the year except Christmas day."

As of 2020, Loveday produced more than 2.7 million kilograms of mushrooms per year.

ON MY SECOND day, a cheerful Black supervisor led the new pickers to the punch card machine, halfway down the long hallway of picking rooms where we would be clocking in for the day. Our next destination was a quality control table, where he dealt out a series of laminated circles on the stainless steel:

- button
- small
- small medium
- medium
- large medium
- large
- jumbo

The supervisor named each size as he dealt them out. I tried to focus on what he was saying instead of being distracted by all the experienced pickers hustling by, racing to get one of the newer carts and then wheeling said cart over to their crew's first room.

We would have to be able to recognize all these sizes, as mushrooms are picked to order. Different vendors want different sizes of mushrooms. One container was for mediums, for instance, and another for larges.

We would also have to be able to recognize and sort by grade. Number ones were smooth unblemished mushrooms with no gills showing. Number twos were blemished or weirdly shaped or that had some gills showing. Threes were mushrooms whose caps were completely open or that were bruised or had knife marks.

The supervisor shuffled and dealt out the circles again, quizzing us on which was which. It was like a strange game of memory, guessing and then turning over the circles to see if we were right. After a few minutes of this, the supervisor walked away, telling us to test each other. We looked at each other, strangers with faces obscured by surgical masks, hair confined to hairnets and covered with helmets, and hands covered by blue latex gloves, shrugged and began.

"Medium? No, small medium. Argh! Small!"

"Large? *Yessssss*."

As you might expect, it was easiest to identify button and jumbo, being smallest and largest. It was harder to know who would make it through the three weeks of training to a spot on one of Loveday's picking crews.

I HAVE THREE degrees, in English, Biology and Journalism. But I have little to no practical skills. I can pound a nail into a wall and hang a picture and I can paint the wall the picture is hanging on, but that's about it.

I often joke that my main talents are carrying heavy things, writing poetry and my enthusiasm for the world.

My longest job to date combined all three: working as a publicist for a book publisher. I hefted boxes of books from our basement warehouse to my car to book tables at conferences where I would burble about our titles to anyone who would listen, and I (sometimes) wrote poetry when I was supposed to be working. (Friends, don't let anyone tell you that writing a press release is the same as writing poetry . . .)

For a few weeks in the fall of 2020, I worked part time as a labourer for my CSA farmer, Jonathan's Farm. CSA stands for Community Supported Agriculture and what it means is that you pay a farmer for an entire season of veg in advance, with weekly pickups of whatever's in season. You trust that farmer to produce an entire season of veg, come hell or high water. Since he farms in Manitoba, that should be come drought or floodwater, because you can have both in a single season these days.

I didn't necessarily need the money, but I wanted to test myself, to throw myself against a wall of hard work. I was restless from a year or more of working from home, from my neighbourhood and my city. I was bored with sitting for a living. It seemed weird to me that my work was mostly inside on a screen and that if I didn't take my body for a walk before/after work, I'd have the aches and pains of inactivity to deal with.

I was forty-seven years old. I like walking and tennis and karate, but I was getting slower and creakier as I got older. But I'm also six feet tall and substantially built and I've always enjoyed the strength that came from this body, the reach it allowed me. I've even allowed myself a few macho handshakes with men who thought it would be fun to squeeze my hand, which is to say: I would squeeze the bejesus out of their hand right back and enjoy the flinches. And I uniformly resist any man who tries to take a box or a bale from me, on the grounds that it's big and heavy and I'm a woman.

Speaking of macho: I'm 255 pounds. Which means that two thousand pounds of mushrooms is only 7.84 of me. And I lug that beautiful weight around all the time.

My first day at Jonathan's Farm, I prepped cured garlic for sale at the farmers' market, sitting and brushing away the extra/dirty husks. By the end of the day, my hands were cramped and my back hurt. But I also hurt after subsequent days spent weeding two/three rows of carrots and then picking melons or harvesting potatoes and then weighing and sorting said melons. Basically, it all hurt.

Some of Jonathan's employees were like me, older and interested in organic farming, in trading labour for food; others were young, looking for outside work while stuck at home, their lives on hold because of the pandemic. But Jonathan had some superhuman employees, all women, that had been with him for years, who could work twelve-hour days without complaining. They knew the work and were strong. I could get stronger and faster, but I already knew I wouldn't get any younger. And I clearly wasn't superhuman.

My clearest memory of that time is from late September. Here's what I posted to Facebook: "So I spent the day at Jonathan's Farm, cleaning/sorting onions. Part of that work was hauling fifty-pound bags of onions through the greenhouse [where they were curing] to the truck. Me and another woman loaded the truck ourselves. I may not be in great shape, but I am big and strong and I love that about my body. I brought home a single onion but also some extra lettuce, kale, melon and leek. I want to make potato leek soup but first I neeeeeeed to haul myself out of the bath."

Jonathan commented: "That was some impressive hauling! 4,000 lb of onions."

If we're using me as a unit of weight, that's only 15.68 Ariels, but I still felt like a giant among (wo)men.

When I started at Loveday a year later, I had been playing tennis and walking in Assiniboine Forest and mudlarking a lot. I felt strong.

I AM HARVESTER 2146. My knife is D46.

It sounds like I'm a character from Frank Herbert's *Dune*, except substitute compost spiked with spawn for sand, room after room of compost- and peat-filled beds for the desert, and mushrooms for spice. Except I'm not a white saviour: I'm not here to overthrow the colonial landlords or even to unionize the workplace.

I'm just interested in all things mushroom.

After twenty years going mushrooming, to photograph and to eat, I wanted to understand the difference between wild and farmed mushrooms. Like many people, I learn best by doing things or by watching other people do things, so I applied for a harvester job at Loveday, which I'd known about since childhood.

Still, everyone inside and outside the factory, co-workers and friends and acquaintances, wanted to know "Why on *earth?!*" I was there.

WHAT I LOVE about mushroom picking is half to do about the mushrooms and half about the culture of picking mushrooms.

First: Number ones, lined up in a tray, look impossibly perfect, like a carton of eggs or a tray of rising dough portioned out.

Second: It is super satisfying to look down a bed and see big mushrooms just waiting for you and your knife. The best is spotting a perfect mushroom at the back of the bed. The back is also the back for the picker on the opposite side of the bed, so you're supposed to respect that boundary and so only pick from your half of the back. But I have the wingspan of a blue-footed booby. Also, I have never had a mammogram, but I practised by mashing my boob against the side of the bed for an extra few inches of reach. You reach and reach and feel it against your fingertips and then it is in your hand, it is yours, and you slice the lower third of the stem off and put it in your tray. And reach for another.

Third: I love the knife rituals. It feels sacred. I also sort of like that we are all armed, though I would be the first one killed in an actual knife fight, being slow/unwilling to hurt people or believe that anyone wanted to hurt me. My real weapon in a fight would be knocking the person down and sitting on them until they calmed down.

Every time break is called, we set down our knives and leave our carts, stripping off our gloves. We wash our hands at the row of sinks that divides the break room from the factory floor. When break is over, we wash our hands again and dry them under a bank of high-powered dryers, the kind that push your skin around. Lisa tapes memos she wants people to read to those dryers. One of them is a list of missing knives.

The knives have to be checked in every night, after being washed and sterilized. If you drop your knife on the floor, if you set it down on your cart and it is jiggled and falls to the floor, you have to go sterilize it again. You have to know where your knife is at all times, because if you leave it in a tray of mushrooms that somehow gets sent to the store without being noticed, there will be *big trouble.*

Fourth: A mushroom farm is like a mall in that it could be any time of the night or day. There are no windows. Every room is the exact same except for the number and size of mushrooms present. There is only you, the mushrooms, your knife and the cart that holds your trays. Tied to the cart's handle is a bag holding multiple pairs of gloves and a roll of labels with your number. You have to put on a new pair of gloves when the ones you are wearing get dirty or torn or when you touch the ground or come back from a break. You pull the cart along, kicking a plastic bucket between the cart and the bed to catch the trimmings. You pick and cut and sort the mushrooms by size, then pull/pull/kick the lot down the row. And that is everything for level two, which you can easily pick standing up. Level one, the level closest to the ground, is picked from a perch on an inverted milk crate or a bucket and is more pulled/scooched/kicked.

Fifth: I love being around mushrooms. I love the knob of mycelia and peat moss that comes up when I pick them. I love the pins – or baby mushrooms – that I relentlessly trim away with the bottom third of the stem.

Back in training, Lisa told us that mushrooms double in size in twenty-four hours. And I believe it. When I'm picking a whole row, when I've gotten to the end and I'm walking back to make sure I haven't missed anything – because the trainers will find anything I've missed – suddenly all the mushrooms that I didn't pick because they were too small are big enough. I don't know if it's because it's been a couple of hours since I decided to leave them and they've grown since or because my sorting brain hasn't fully calibrated to mushroom sizes. I wish I could hear them growing, the way I can sometimes hear the grassy sound of release as the mushroom is separated from the mycelia and the peat moss of the bed.

Sixth: I love that my number is written on the top of my plastic hard hat. I love that when a supervisor doesn't know your name, or they're wading into a dispute, they start yelling a few feet away: "Sister! *Sisterrrrrrrrrr!*" The new pickers have adopted it, so I'm hearing Cantonese- and Punjabi- and Somali-inflected versions, said in friendly and frustrated tones. I love listening to people speaking Punjabi and Cantonese and Somali and probably half a dozen other languages in the hallway and in the break room. I can duck under the sound and inhabit a timeless space.

Seventh: For once in my goddamn life, I'm not multi-tasking. I'm not trying to write and do laundry and clean the kitchen and make sure my daughter has something to eat after getting home from school. Answering emails, checking in with friends. Writing intermixed with editing and submissions and grant writing. And with my phone back in my locker, with no clock to watch in the picking rooms, I'm not distracted. I'm surprised every time our trainers, Bin and Jasmit, call break, though you could literally set your watch by it, stopping every hour and a half.

Bin says that if I work there long enough, my body will tell me when it's break time. If I get hungry or thirsty, it's probably break time. I notice that the other pickers, the experienced ones, eat at every break. They have enormous lunch bags from which they take elaborate home-cooked meals that I covet, the same way I covet the Filipino picnics, set out in big foil trays on picnic tables, every time I go to one of Winnipeg's big parks on summer weekends.

WILD MUSHROOMS HAD been everywhere in September, after a week of rain wetted down woodlands and boulevards that were desperately dry after months of drought.

That rain was followed by a few days of sunny temps, which meant we had a *muchness* of mushrooms. In Assiniboine Forest, there were aspen boletes (*Leccinum insigne*) or shaggy scalycaps (*Pholiota squarrosa*) under trembling aspens, coral mushrooms on decaying logs and elm oysters on Manitoba maples. On the boulevard, there were velvet foot and shaggy manes and inky cap mushrooms everywhere. It was glorious.

We'd had a very warm first half of October with temps as high as 28°C on October 6, but by the end of the month, when I started at Loveday, it had cooled down. There was frost most mornings.

Mushrooming outside was done, but it was always an uncertain proposition at best. Sometimes I would find edible mushrooms that I could ID with certainty, but they were either too young and not worth picking or too old and full of bugs. Sometimes I'd find only beautiful toxic species. And sometimes, after hours of walking in the woods, I wouldn't find anything, the ground too wet or too dry. But I could always find mushrooms at Loveday.

And while I was used to picking a few pounds at most in the wild, not a hundred or more pounds per day, I was just happy to see mushrooms again.

THE OTHER THING most people want to know is if the factory smells.

It doesn't. The air smells faintly of peat, of mushrooms, but since the mushrooms are picked when immature and the rooms are climate controlled and kept on the cool side, it is negligible. But I have almost no sense of smell, so one day I asked Sagal, a young Somali Muslim woman, as we waited to be told which room we'd go to next, if the picking rooms smelled bad to her.

Sagal said everyone asked her the same thing, which confused her, because like me, she could detect no smells.

I think that's a question from people who live in the northeast section of the city now or who grew up in Winnipeg. When I was a kid, driving along Lagimodière in the northeastern section of the city or near industrial St. Boniface was a stinky proposition. There was an egg factory from which my mother sometimes picked up a flat of eggs and I used to sit in the back seat, stunned by the reek, which seemed to be everywhere but especially all the way up my nose.

I asked on Facebook if anyone knew what the components of the stink were, then and now. "Boiled meat, rotting meat, meat meal, offal, manure, tar, burnt rubber," commented Bertrand Nayet, poet and co-founder of nearly all the Franco-Manitoban literary institutions.

Marianne Cerilli, who was an NDP MLA from 1990 until 2003 of the Radisson constituency, said that among the contributors to the smell were a slaughterhouse and an oil refinery. She added that while she was in office, the NDP stopped two additional hog slaughter and packing plants from being constructed in the area.

"Transcona and St. Boniface have a lot of contaminated sites," Cerilli noted. "There are a lot of land use conflicts between residential and industrial uses that bring residents into close proximity to noise pollution, air pollution, soil contamination and noxious odours."

Back then, Loveday's Mission Street location would have contributed to the reek, given that the substrate it grew its mushrooms from was compost made from hay, straw and chicken manure. But that started to change in the late '80s, when Loveday upgraded their operations. That boosted both the amount of compost and mushrooms they were able to produce at the Mission Street plant. But until 2003, compost was still being produced outside. That year they moved the composting operation from outdoor ricks to indoor bunkers: "A new, 7,920 square foot concrete structure with three composting chambers was built. Each chamber features a powerful fan that pumps huge amounts of fresh air through the compost heaps. Computer-controlled sensors constantly monitor temperatures and oxygen levels in the heaps. The technology, with its shorter composting cycles and virtual elimination of anaerobic conditions, has resulted in greater control of process odours."

From 2003 to 2007, Loveday invested more than three million dollars on these kinds of upgrades, to help reduce the odours "emanating" from their Mission Street plant.

WHEN I'M PICKING, my brain is a good engine, humming down the beds. I am quieted, consumed by pick-cut-put.

Mostly, it's just me and the mushrooms. Quiet, just the white noise of the ventilation system and my breath. Today, I can hear the Somali pickers across the aisle chatting. I can hear the trainer, Bin, walk up and start commenting on their mushrooms, trying to get them to pick properly. Both our trainers, Bin and Jasmit, are new in this role, freshly promoted from picking, and Bin sometimes gets frustrated, though I think he's genuinely trying to help them.

I don't think Hawa, the older Somali woman, can read English. I don't think she can read the order on the door of each room, so she's watching what other people are picking. But every room is different: sometimes it's a pick-off, where you pick everything except garbage and pins. Sometimes we pick all sizes into one box. And sometimes we're supposed to leave the smalls and mediums, so there will be mediums and larges the next day.

I wish I could translate for Hawa. Bin is trying, but he speaks Cantonese-accented English and Jasmit speaks Punjabi-accented English. Sometimes Sagal comes and translates, but she's trying to earn money too, to learn and get quicker at picking, and she's

already being pulled away to translate fairly often. I can imagine
what Hawa is feeling, trying and failing to understand the new
English words and then to recognize them again coming out of
Bin's and Jasmit's mouths. She seems to mostly be picking the same
thing every time in mixed boxes, which makes Bin's blood boil.

Hawa also seems to be insisting on her own terminology. Tiny
instead of button, large large instead of jumbo.

I can hear people in the room next to us chatting, calling back
and forth to each other, to the runners, laughing. I haven't been close
enough to anyone that speaks good-enough English to chat like that
while I'm picking. A Somali man in my crew has been singing – a lul-
laby, I think – which is kind of nice, reminding me of being sung to
by my mother, of singing to my own daughter. This morning, before
I finish my row and go to the next room, we are joined by a crew of
mostly Cantonese-speaking pickers, who have been assigned to pick
the upper rows. And one of them starts singing too.

ONE DAY, I asked Bin, "If you were a mushroom, which one would
you be?" I said I would be a number two: a bit weird and bumpy,
but still perfectly good. Bin immediately said he was a number
one, then took a second or two to decide on the size: medium. (I
asked Jasmit the next day: she said it was a funny question.)

I LOVE MUSHROOMS whether or not they're edible. I love everything about them: the way they look, the way they feel, where and
how they grow.

I don't normally eat that many *Agaricus bisporus*. For me,
they're like white meat on a turkey: it's too much work to make
them worth eating. Which is to say: browning them in butter and
garlic or steaming them in broth.

If I'm going to eat mushrooms, I prefer more flavourful ones like wild lobster mushrooms and the rarer morels or ones with nicer textures like oyster mushrooms, foraged, grow-kitted or bought.

One day, waiting to hear what our next picking room will be, one of the trainees asks if we ate mushrooms regularly. The Somali matriarch of our training group says that they don't really eat mushrooms in her culture. Jasmit looks up and down the hall and says that she didn't eat mushrooms much before she started at Loveday and now she definitely won't. I make a similar confession, but don't mention that over the course of the pandemic, my family had been trying out more vegetarian options. We figured out a way that we all liked tofu – the secret? Cornstarch! – added Japanese curry blocks to our repertoire and started regularly roasting portobellos – which are just large *Agaricus bisporus* – with breadcrumbs, herbs and oil. My daughter says she doesn't like eating mushrooms, probably to break my heart, so the portobellos are just for me.

I WAIT UNTIL I've worked at Loveday for a week before I mention it on social media, posting a picture of me in my helmet, hairnet and mask.

I knew that most of the middle-income people on my feed would have one question: "Why? You can make more money at a desk job. You made more money at the desk job you just quit."

What does it mean to be a class traitor? The last time, I was a security guard, first for the Pan Am Games mainstage, working the evening shift. I was twenty-six, newly returned from teaching ESL in Seoul, South Korea, and I wanted to see if I could live cheaply and only work part time. The rest of the time, I would write. When the games finished, I worked weekends at the Cargill building and the people signing in at the lobby desk would look at me quizzically, ask what I was doing there.

"Are you a student?" they would ask.

"No," I'd answer. I always tried to leave it at that, but when the quizzical looks stretched on too long, I would add, "I'm a writer."

This time, I hesitate to mention that I am working for Loveday. Now that I'm forty-eight and fully settled in my writing career, most people avoid asking why, because *clearly* I'm committed to my economic instability. And I don't want to say that I took the job as a lark so that I could write about it, even though that is at least partly true. Like with Jonathan's Farm, I think I wanted to see if I could do it, as a middle-aged person in reasonably okay shape.

I also wanted to dignify the labour, though most of my jobs to date had been in offices. As a publicist, planning and promoting launches and book tours meant entire days in front of a screen, typing a whole range of cheerful/persuasive emails: "C'mon! I *know* you want to review this title/interview this author/partner with us on this book launch/write this promo piece for me!!" Some days, it felt like I was perched on my keyboard like a vulture, typing with my fingers and toes. The idea was to soar, to help our authors be in conversation with everyone and anyone, but most days it felt like I was just barely aloft.

It's worth noting that no one ever mentions that most of the entry-level jobs in arts admin or book publishing – the dream jobs of English grads everywhere – pay only fifteen or seventeen dollars per hour after a university degree, which isn't that much of an improvement on minimum wage with no qualifications.

No one mentions that the arts are built on the backs and shoulders of educated/eager young women, willing to work for almost nothing. No one mentions parents or spouses providing what those jobs can't: rent/grocery money, health insurance.

FOR AN ENTIRE week, I only see the outside when I emerge from the factory at 3:32 p.m. and drive home, drinking water, tallying up what hurts during rush hour and then weekend traffic. I let Irish Siri choose the fastest route and I choose the music. It turns out, Irish Siri likes industrial parks. But I am too tired to notice or care, so I just turn when she says to turn, only watching the traffic lights and the cars in front of and behind me.

Every day when I get home, I immediately shower or take a bath, applying hot water to my sore shoulders/back/legs/feet. Then I lie in bed for a while, amazed that I'm not moving. Sometimes I fall asleep, only waking up at what normally would be my bedtime. Other times, I get up, eat something and watch some TV. But I don't go out – it is a series of insides all week.

And it is so strange – entering that factory was like entering the fairylands. The time inside is endless and uncounted, while the outside world continues as it has. I don't make any plans for the future, don't think about things that are troubling me – I just reach for a mushroom, then another, in the day and night of the underhill.

WHAT PEOPLE ARE really asking, when they're asking why I took this job, is: "Why aren't you doing better-paid and less physically demanding work?"

The reason people go to university is so that they can get white-collar jobs in offices. Blue-collar jobs, especially unskilled ones like harvesting mushrooms, are hard on the body over the long term. And what happens when you get sick or your body starts to wear out?

In Manitoba, as in the rest of Canada, the hardest and dirtiest jobs, at farms and slaughterhouses and factories, are often taken by temporary foreign workers, by newcomers to Canada and lower-income people who can't afford to attend university, who don't have a support network.

Now I don't see every single person every single day, but I am pretty sure I am the only Canadian-born white harvester during my shifts among the sixty-plus people working in that role most days. Some of the other harvesters give me the side eye when they first see me. Others come around a corner and startle because I am a white person – a big white person – and a woman. I am told more than once that at first they thought I was Marsha, a white manager who was on leave from Loveday while I was there.

I expected this job to be about exploring the difference between the woods and a factory, natural and unnatural mushrooms, but instead, like everything, it is about race and class.

I WASN'T SURE I would, but I like picking mushrooms for a living. I like learning a room, an aisle, a row of twelve beds up and down. I like filling trays with the proscribed size of mushrooms. I like the weird misshapen mushrooms that are automatically number twos. I like the hint of pink gill of a freshly opened number two and the brown gills and squishy cap of an older one.

What is hard is being all alone in a crowded break room. The first two days, I have Tammy, an Indigenous woman who started the same day I did. We chat and sip water from our water bottles, and sometimes Sagal joins us, even though her mother and aunts are around. And then Tammy stops coming. Maybe she didn't like the work, maybe she found a better job somewhere else, but all I know is that I miss her.

The third day is the worst, because one woman brings out a big bag full of samosas at lunchtime and hands them out to what seems like everyone but me. I packed myself a good lunch but I have never wanted a samosa *more*.

By lunchtime on the fifth day, it is too much, so I go and sit with Bin, hoping he'll talk to me. But he is too young to understand what I want: conversation, acknowledgement. Maybe if he was older, he would have understood. But that isn't entirely fair: it is supposed to be his break too, to take off his new managerial persona the way the rest of us take off our masks.

The last time I was surrounded by people but completely silent for an extended period was the first two weeks of university. I was the only one to come to the University of Winnipeg from my graduating class at a small French-immersion high school and I knew no one, so the only people I interacted with directly where the cafeteria ladies, who served me plates of fries or rung up my mugs of teas. I was so grateful for them, in those first few weeks and in the years afterward, when I would study in the cafeteria.

I chat with a few other trainees at the end of my shift, which is nice. But mostly I spend the week listening to other people. Loveday is a noisy place – people calling down the long hallway, people chatting while they pick, people joking with each other in the break room – but I am shut out, linguistically and socially. Mostly I spend the week listening to the mushrooms release from the mycelia that tie them to the beds and to Bin and Jasmit cajoling/ordering/convincing our roomful of new pickers to do things "the right way."

On the first day of picking, I drop my knife four or five times, which means five trips to the knife station. I just don't know where to put my knife when I'm not picking. The second and third days, I drop it maybe two or three times. By day five, I realize that the best place to leave my knife isn't on my cart but plunged deep into the peat/compost/mycelia where I am picking. The bright-orange handle makes it easy to spot and there is no danger of it falling to the floor. On the fifth day, I drop my knife once and that is a fluke. But at least I don't dump any mushrooms, unlike one trainee who dumps a box of mushrooms twice, sighing heavily.

MY STINTS AT Jonathan's Farm and Loveday had something else in common: I pregamed with anti-inflammatories. My logic? "If you stay ready, you don't have to get ready," a tidbit of wisdom the Internet attributes to Will Smith or Conor McGregor or Dejuan Walker.

I'm not pain-free until the third week. And then they up the ante, training us on the lifts, which allow pickers to access the third to fifth levels of the mushroom beds. The movements for the lifts – attaching them to the rails that allow you to wheel from one end to the other like a librarian in a fancy library, climbing up, then picking from them – are completely different. But I am only ever up on the lifts for a few hours. The heights don't bother me for a few hours. It feels like an adventure, especially as someone who has been restricted to the first two rows – standing and then sitting – for three weeks.

The fourth week is where everything goes wrong. For my first shift as a real picker, I am on the lifts for eight hours straight. My body starts to hurt in new and different ways and after the first day, I start to dislike picking from heights. I feel unbalanced. What's more, I feel the impatience from the experienced pickers with my slowness, though I've already met and exceeded the company's picking goal for the first month: twenty pounds an hour. So I try to speed up, which means I make more mistakes.

After two days of getting so frustrated I cry – the first day in the hallway, after Jasmit asks how it was going and looks deeeeeeep into my eyes, and the second, hiding in the washroom – I realize that I'm not learning anything anymore. I am just getting overwhelmed. It will take me months to get fast enough to earn real money, to get fitter and stronger. I'm not superhuman, like those awesome women at Jonathan's Farm.

In the end, I realize that I don't have to keep working at Loveday, that I can go back to a white-collar job or maybe find something that falls between a white and blue. Off-white? Acid-wash blue?

I had been pushing so hard to make it through the first few weeks of training, where everything was physically demanding. Every week I would count down the days, waiting for my days off, and that got me through. But working in a real crew is emotionally and physically demanding. I am nearly fifty years old, weeping in a bathroom stall.

And once I realize that I don't have to work there anymore, that I can stop, I can't persuade myself to go back.

In retrospect, I'm sad I didn't try to tough it out for another week or two. To prove to myself and to the other pickers that I could make it in a real crew, instead of being reasonably good/fast on a training crew.

I'm sad that I didn't get to thank Bin and Jasmit for all their help, for their gentle friendship. I'm sad that I didn't stay long enough to see Hawa succeed.

THE ONLY SECRET I take away from Loveday, though it's an open secret, is that all the mushrooms that they currently produce are organic.

"This entire farm is organic . . . but maybe 15 percent of what we grow here actually gets sold as organic," Burton Loveday noted in that 2014 interview. "Even though the other 85 percent we grow here is organic, it doesn't go out under an organic label."

The reason that Loveday's mushrooms are all organic regardless of label is that all their growing was moved to the new facility in Springfield, Manitoba, in 2010. The 73,000-square-foot facility is certified pesticide- and fungicide-free, with regular monitoring and certified cleaning products. So you can buy the ones labelled "organic" or the ones that aren't, that may or may not be cheaper on a given day, but they're all organic.

Xmas tree farmers encourage their customers to reuse and recycle their Xmas trees but they don't control whether municipalities have programs to mulch Xmas trees or if people use them for winter bird shelter in their yards. Mushroom farmers, on the other hand, use hay, straw and chicken manure, which are products and by-products of grain and chicken farms, for their compost. And while they use peat – which is starting to be recognized as an unsustainable product, despite its utility to gardeners and farmers – to layer on top of the compost, it is reused when the fungi have gotten to the end of their life cycle. In Loveday's case, Reimer Soils picks up the trimmings and mushroom garbage (too old/weird/fell on the floor) as well as the used compost/peat from the beds. They use this to create what they call Organic Soil Enhancer or "spent mushroom compost" that will "add valuable nutrients, and improve the physical condition of your soil and its ability to process air and water."

In a 2021 article by Efficiency Manitoba, detailing energy-efficient upgrades to the Springfield farm, Burton Loveday reflected on the nature of mushroom farming: "Mushroom farming is by nature recycling or taking waste products or byproducts of agriculture and turning it into a food product. So being more energy efficient is just a natural follow-through of that process."

SPEAKING OF NATURAL follow-throughs, in the eight weeks before I started at Loveday, the irritable bowel syndrome I'd gotten rid of years before had been slowly creeping back. Which meant constipation, followed by cramps and then diarrhea. Five weeks in, I started taking probiotic supplements, which had helped before.

But do you know what I really needed? To eat/drink and def-ecate/urinate on a set schedule. It took two and a half weeks of working at Loveday – of breaks every hour and a half, where I ate something, drank something and used the washroom – for my poops to return to normal. I think the light constant activity that is picking mushrooms probably also had something to do with it.

It turns out that my body is a machine that likes to be filled/emptied regularly. I also found that I was more attuned to when I was hungry and when I was full. In my usual life, I eat at irregular times. I sometimes eat because I'm bored or when I'm offered a treat. I sometimes skip meals and then find myself incapacitated by a hunger headache.

The best part of my mushroom-picking day was saving an apple and a cookie or even half a cookie and eating them on the drive home. The second-best part of my day was opening the door to leave the factory and seeing what kind of day it was outside, having arrived in the icy dark.

Not all the changes that mushroom picking introduced to my daily rhythms were good: in the weeks before I started, I spent all kinds of time outside. Partly that was because I knew I needed to exercise my body and outside activities are free. Partly it was because I am happiest in nature. But in my first week at Loveday I saw the outside only when driving home. I was surprised in some ways that it still existed, after the no-time of the factory, of the picking rooms. I didn't go for a single walk that whole time – I went from my house to the factory, from the shower to my bed. I was sore that first week, but not as sore as I could have been. Those few weeks of intense outdoor activities had prepared me physically, but I still missed the outdoors, the elated aimlessness, the connection to the world I felt there.

There was a calm and purpose to picking mushrooms that I still miss. If I had to pick between an hour of office work and an hour of mushroom picking at the same wage, I think I'd choose mushroom picking. But it isn't one hour – it's eight or ten or twelve hours. It's the expectation that my pounds per hour rate would always be increasing.

I still miss mushroom picking, or maybe just me in those long cool single-minded rooms, but it didn't leave much room for anything else. My daughter complained that she hardly saw me, complained when I went out on my days off. And I spent a lot of time when not working feeling dormant. I could sit around, watching TV or reading, but I wasn't good for much of anything that required concentration and energy.

I left with respect for my fellow pickers and a determination to eat more mushrooms.

MY LAST WEEK at Loveday, Bin told me the story of Moon, a female picker who is super fast and who apparently doesn't eat anything, drink anything or go to the bathroom during her shifts. Moon is more than just superhuman: she's godlike.

I couldn't imagine being able to work eight or ten hours at full speed without any of those inputs and outputs. Three weeks in, I still couldn't imagine working more than eight hours *with* them, even though eight hours of work is a luxury afforded only to trainees.

There was a moment of silence between us as we walked down the long hallway toward the break room. Then I told Bin that he was right, that I'm a machine that likes to be filled and emptied at regular intervals.

He laughed and said, "That means you're not a machine."

Cultivator

IN THE EARLY days of the pandemic, my daughter force-fed me a diet of *Hannibal* episodes, sometimes as many as three a night. The 2013 TV series takes up Thomas Harris's stories of a bon-vivant psychiatrist who is ALSO a cannibal serial killer.

Having run through all three seasons by the end of November 2020, I spent the next few months rewatching particular scenes and episodes over Anna's shoulder, mostly the ones between Will Graham (as played by Hugh Dancy) and Hannibal Lecter (as played by Mads Mikkelsen).

She ships 'Hannigram' and so has been revisiting the moments of tenderness/tension between them, many of which involve a knife to the abdomen or, in one instance, a surgical saw to the head. She likes it because of the doomed relationship, I think, but also because Hannibal flouts all kinds of taboos – killing people, eating people – with ease and even, dare I say it, élan.

Hannibal the Cannibal spends the three seasons of the show persuading Will, an FBI special agent whose main talent is being able to empathize with serial killers, to not only empathize with him but to become like him, to join him.

And, maybe, to love him.

CLOSE TO XMAS, my dad's wife texts to say that she has a mushroom kit for me.

The last gift I received from Allison was a little pouch with a handful of my dad's ashes this past summer. I like to think I am not sentimental, but I keep it/him next to the plants I dragged home from the office when the pandemic hit.

The pouch is made of off-white leather and is triangular, with a zipper up one side. If you handle it too much, the fine ashes are sifted through the top of the zipper, like flour.

One of my sisters refused to take her allocation of ashes, her face creased with distress, both pale and flushed. She didn't like the idea of it, didn't want or need it.

That day, we walked down to the old single-lane bridge that in my father's day accommodated cars but now only knows the feet of people eating ice cream from the Bridge Drive-In on the other side while they look at the silty river.

We – my dad's wife, my stepsister, my half-sister, my two full sisters and I – crossed the bridge, something each of us had probably done dozens of times, separately and together.

On the walk over, I looked at the patterns of light and shadow on the bridge, on the backs and shoulders of my siblings. I thought about all the ways we were connected and all the ways we were isolated.

On the other side, we descended to the riverbank slowly, in ones and twos, but before we had all arrived, Allison had emptied one of the pouches. Some of the ashes caught on the breeze, so I turned my head, not wanting to ingest fine particles of my father.

In December, Allison texted to see if I would be home, not wanting to leave the mushroom kit, with its living mycelium, on my porch to freeze.

It was probably the best gift I got that contactless Xmas.

HANNIBAL FINISHED AIRING in August 2015. It was well on its way to becoming a cult classic, but in June 2020, Netflix added it to their catalogue. It found a new, content-hungry audience, so much so that for a while it seemed like a fourth season might be in the works.

I watched the show with Anna because it was one of the few shows she'd watch with me. So it didn't matter, precisely, if I liked *Hannibal*: it was a way to spend time with her. But I came to love its lavish production values – the food! the clothes! the furniture! – and how heavily upholstered the dialogue was. It had the compression of poetry, sometimes. Other times it veered toward, crashed into, absurdity.

My daughter told me that someone on her social media said that if you just thought of the characters as stoned vampires, it made more sense.

A MUSHROOM GROW kit is a plastic bag filled with mycelium-infested sawdust.

The bag is dumpy, more like a ten-pound bag of potatoes than a bag of flour. But to make the comparison perfect, it would have to be one enormous potato. To make the comparison terrible, the bag is the same size as a broad-chested toddler. Lifting it onto the counter is like hoisting a kid from the floor to your hip or into the kitchen sink for a bath. (I never bathed Anna this way, but she stood on our bathroom vanity most nights when she was a toddler, getting her wispy blond hair blow-dried.)

The bag is gathered at the top with a metal clip and has a square notch or vent near the top. If the bag was an abdomen, the vent is where the suprasternal notch, that gap between the clavicles, would be.

I have to find somewhere for this baby to perch. It doesn't need light or heat, like a plant, but it needs space and moisture.

OF ALL THE outrageous serial killers featured on *Hannibal*, I was most intrigued by Eldon Stammets, featured in the second episode of the first season, dubbed "Amuse-Bouche."

Stammets is a serial killer who specializes in diabetics.

He uses his day job as a pharmacist to target diabetic customers, giving them the wrong medication. This switcheroo increases the chance that they'll go into ketoacidosis, which can lead to coma and even death. Stammets then abducts the comatose diabetics, takes them out to a state park and buries them in what the forensics team characterizes as a "highly concentrated mixture of hardwoods, shredded newspaper and pig poop."

Basically, Stammets is turning diabetics into mushroom grow kits.

Showrunner Bryan Fuller explained the genesis of this killer on the AV Club website:

Scott Nimerfro, who is one of our writers, said, "Well, wouldn't it be interesting if he was burying people to grow mushrooms on them?" and then we started doing mushroom research and found this TED Talk by a mycelium expert named Stamets, who we named the character after and thought, "Oh hey, what if this guy had lost his rocker?" Not only fell off, but completely lost it and thought that because mycelium and human beings share a lot of central kind of functions, physiologically, that what if you wanted to blend those two or connect those two? And if he was looking for a connection, isn't that kind of paralleling what Hannibal and Will are going through on their story?

Fuller was referring to American mycologist and mushroom guru Paul Stamets, who, in addition to his books and fungi-based R&D, sells mushroom supplements via his website.

This wasn't the last time that Stamets was the basis for a character on a TV show. On *Star Trek: Discovery*, which started airing in 2017, the USS *Discovery* is powered by a spore drive that is managed by astromycologist Paul Stamets.

MY FRIEND YVONNE Blomer is a poet with diabetes who lives in Victoria.

We talk most days. She saves me not from serial killers but from loneliness and ennui. We have done several book tours together and so, when I heard that she'd bought a small RV, my main thought was "RV-based book tours! Huzzah!" It was February and cold when she messaged me to say that she'd found mushrooms growing in her RV, knowing my interest in all things fungal.

I woke up and was feeling around my head in the bunk bed, above the driver's seat, in our RV, for my book, glasses, socks, etc . . . and I felt a thing and I was like, What the heck is that? And then I looked and it was a rather large mushroom. White with a wide stalk and a smallish cap. It felt quite yucky. I freaked a tiny bit and got out of bed and sent my husband to look. We of course instantly worried about leaking water and I then blamed the dog for bringing spores to my bed. I could see a light dusting on the mattress, so borrowed a vacuum from my sister, as we were parked in her driveway on our way up island. We had nothing to patch the leak or anything else so just cleaned it, got bleach cloths and wiped and hoped more wouldn't grow.

Even weeks later, Yvonne was freaked out by the mushroom, which she described as being the size of a child's fist.

"My armpits tingle just thinking about it," she said. "It was a very rubbery feeling mushroom. My sister thought it was quite funny."

Yvonne's next step, after removing the offending mushroom/spores?

To google the phrase "mushrooms in my RV," so I thought it was only fair to do the same and then gorge myself on the horrifying/home-wrecking images that appeared.

ANNA IS A child of the Internet, so she was able to get me a copy of the "Amuse-Bouche" script.

Eleven pages in (or 10:40 into the episode, if you prefer), three boys, described as Wildlife Explorers, discover nine bodies in the woods at Elk Neck State Park in Maryland. The shallow graves are covered in enormous clusters of mushrooms and each features an arm sticking out of the grave, propped up by rebar and attached to medical tubing that provided the comatose but not-quite-dead victims with dextrose. Stammets intended to keep his victims alive for a while after he interred them, but by the time they're discovered, six of seven are dead.

Once the FBI forensics team moves in, the small clearing is full of mushroom-infested bodies. The mushrooms are huge and creamy-white, growing on top of but also out of the sides of the bodies.

It is a beautiful/terrible sight. The strangeness of the scene is highlighted when FBI agent Beverly Katz quips, "You find any shiitakes?" Oh! Right! People forage in wild spaces like state parks for mushrooms.

I wonder: Would these mushrooms, grown on/from human bodies, be safe to eat? This is an appropriate question for a show about a cannibal who delights in serving unwitting guests elaborate meals made entirely from human meat. Would it be something I would want to eat, like mushrooms foraged from city streets or volunteer tomatoes from the riverbank?

Katz's line isn't in the script, but I love it.

What *is* in the "Amuse-Bouche" script is that the mushrooms growing on the human bodies are *Pleurotus nidiformis*, otherwise known as ghost fungi, though since 2013 the name has shifted to *Omphalotus nidiformis*.

I think that the writers liked the name more than anything else, because that mushroom is native to Australia and Tasmania, *not* Maryland. Usually found growing at the base of eucalyptus trees, it is toxic (though not usually fatal) and bioluminescent.

But the mushrooms in the episode don't appear to be ghost fungi, as they're missing the nestlike structure that is distinctive to the species; also, we don't get a night scene where they're glowing in the dark.

The series was filmed in Canada and the special effects artist for the mushroom corpses, among others, was François Dagenais, with Scarborough's MindWarp Productions. He included a gallery of images from the episode on his online portfolio.

Curious about the gap between the shooting script and what was filmed, I immediately emailed François:

1. The script lists the mushrooms as being *Pleurotus nidiformis*, otherwise known as ghost fungus, a bio-luminescent mushroom that is native to Australia. It doesn't seem like that was the mushroom you used. Can you tell me which mushroom you used as your model? To me, they look like oyster mushrooms . . .

2. Was it difficult to build a human 'grow kit'? What did you use as a reference?

François's assistant replied immediately, saying that François would be in touch. But he's never responded.

Does that mean that I was ghosted while asking about ghost fungi?

I THINK HANNIBAL would appreciate the instructions I got from the grow kit vendor: "Once [the] bag is mostly or fully colonized cut a big X into middle or bottom of bag 3 inches x 3 inches, and place into fruiting conditions."

The prairies are located in the continental climate, which means an extreme range of temperatures between winter and summer: from -40 to +40°C.

Our house is old, built in 1912. Old in this case means drafty, despite our retrofitting, which means that in the winter we struggle to keep the house warm and humid. I run humidifiers in the living room and my bedroom to keep our skin from drying out, our noses from bleeding, and to dissipate the lightning storms of static electricity. (In Victoria's temperate zone, Yvonne tilts her screen to show me the green grass in her backyard. It is January and we have gotten a foot of snow already; I feel a jab of pain.)

Our house is also small, full of people and junk. So there aren't that many pockets I can cordon off in which to create a temperate climate. Also, our cats interfere with plants and anything they think might be edible and/or fit in their mouths, so that means nowhere the cats are.

Which leaves me with closets, our bedroom and the pantry. (The cats want nothing more than access to those spaces, scratching at doors, sticking their paws underneath, lurking in case we accidentally leave doors open . . .)

I've decided to put the grow kit next to the potato bin in the pantry, which is really just a space at the top of the basement stairs where we've jammed shelves and filled them with cans of beans/ extra jars of salsa. I even find a spare dinner plate the bag can rest on, creamy-white like the mycelium.

I'm ready. I should cut a big X, but for some reason I hesitate.

WHEN ELDON STAMMETS has been stopped.

When Eldon Stammets has been shot and is lying on the floor, bleeding, he starts monologuing, which is to say, he explains the method behind his madness. Stammets uses concepts the show's writers paraphrased from Paul Stamets's 2008 Ted Talk, "6 ways mushrooms can save the world." The video of this lecture has been viewed over ten million times on YouTube and TED Talk's website.

"We're more closely related to fungi than we are to any other kingdom," says Paul Stamets, while he paces the stage. "A group of twenty eukaryotic microbiologists published a paper two years ago erecting opisthokonta – a super-kingdom that joins animalia and fungi together." Later, "The mycelium is sentient. It knows that you are there. When you walk across landscapes, it leaps up in the aftermath of your footsteps, trying to grab debris."

Eldon the serial killer/mushroom cultivator believes that he can connect with people only by putting them in the ground and infesting them with mycelia. Do the victims have to be diabetics? Do the mushrooms have to be ghost fungi, imported from Australia?

Probably not, but it's still creepy fun.

I STILL HAVE three small Xs on my abdomen from a 2018 laparoscopic surgery that removed a fluid-filled cyst on my Fallopian tubes that was the size of a small orange.

Sometimes, when I'm changing clothes, I find myself absently tracing the scars to see if they're still there, to teach myself about my changing menopausal body.

I still have a small scar on my spine, close to my bum, from the spina bifida occulta I was born with. I had a mole where the scar is and in my early teens, my mother asked the doctor to look at it. He worried the mole was cancerous, so it was removed. When the biopsy results came back negative, I was sent for imaging, where they learned it was a spina bifida occulta.

I have the most survivable form of spina bifida; with the other types, a fluid-filled sac extrudes from the body. In the worst cases, the spinal cord and nerves are also in the sac.

So when I cut an X into the bag's abdomen, taking care not to cut too small or too big, I wonder: Can you disembowel a mushroom grow kit?

I'm meant to mist the bag with a spray bottle several times daily. But this is the pandemic, so I alternate between tending to the grow kit and ignoring it, especially when our basement sewer outpipes get blocked and poop/ooze from our pipes rises, if only thinly and briefly.

The lesson: if you've got a door you can close on a problem, you do.

But then a lump extruded from the hole.

I THINK THAT episode of *Hannibal* works because it plays on people's fear of wild mushrooms.

The nine human/mushroom grow kits are visually wonderful/terrible, with big cream-coloured mushrooms erupting from bodies as they decayed and became unrecognizable. The oyster mushrooms that Eldon Stammets grew, that I was growing, are saprobic: "Mushrooms that are saprobes survive by decomposing dead or decaying organic material and using it as food," says Michael Kuo of MushroomExpert.com. "Many wood-rotting fungi are saprobes, and help decompose deadwood – but other wood rotters are parasitic and attack living wood."

Kuo notes that, in the forest, oyster mushrooms grow in "shelf-like clusters on dead logs and living trees (primarily hardwoods, but sometimes on conifers); causing a white rot."

That's why oyster mushroom kits consist of sawdust infested with mycelium: it replicates ideal forest conditions.

Incidentally, oyster mushrooms are one of the most sought-after mushrooms for foragers. It helps, I think, that there aren't that many poisonous look-alikes.

Because as the saying goes, every mushroom is edible *once*.

IT TOOK A while for my grow kit to start making mushrooms.

I am someone who for many years thought that "fungi" was a synonym for "mushroom." But that's like saying "apple tree" is a synonym for "apple." The mushroom is the fruiting body of the fungi just like the apple is the fruit of the apple tree. An apple contains seeds. A mushroom contains spores. But the purpose is the same: more apple trees and more fungi, somewhere other than where the original apple tree/fungi are.

According to my instructions, "after about four days baby mushrooms (pins) will form from the slit and grow over the next week, weighing as much as 1-3lb 1st flush."

But I will admit that I doubted, so I turned the bag around and stabbed it again. In the back!

I am mortified when pins start to emerge from the first wound. And then: an enormity of pins from the second!

At some point, I realize that I can't get enough moisture into the bone-dry winter air, so I take a large clear plastic bag from the conglomeration under the sink and drape it around both growths.

I am anxious about ruining it, but I try to tell myself the two tumours are like two apples on a tree, growing and ripening at different rates. As much as I've admired apples as I pulled them down from trees, oyster mushrooms are much more startling, beautiful and strange.

The mushrooms grow exponentially overnight. The caps are a taupe that drifted into a liver-y purple while the stems are a creamy white. I look forward to checking on them every morning and seeing how much they've grown.

It is like a pandemic Advent calendar, outclassing my cheese Advent calendar, because in the latter case every day you got a similarly shaped lump of cheese and eventually the cardboard housing basically disintegrated and then all I had was a handful of individually wrapped lumps of cheeses in my fridge, which was okay, because cheese. Except I hated all the plastic.

The reason I like picking apples is because being half in and half out of an apple tree, my arms above my head, is an activity that is thousands and possibly millions of years old. Most of my other activities, including working on a computer and driving, are a hundred years old or less. I also love how sun-warm apples taste and the smell of a car full of apples. If this essay was an Instagram post, the caption would read: "Best air-freshener EVER!"

Similarly, I like the texture of mushrooms because they're not like anything else I touch: plastic and metal and wood, cotton and polyester and linen. There aren't any other food equivalents for the slightly rubbery feeling, either: vegetables are crisp and watery while meat is dense and wet.

THE SPRING AND summer when Anna was four, I inadvertently became a monarch butterfly rancher. (That's what comes from going to something billed as a 'monarch butterfly festival' and buying a single small milkweed, which apparently had monarch eggs on it . . .)

I spent almost all my free time for four weeks sourcing milkweed in green spaces and gardens (which often *also* had eggs on it, starting the cycle anew) to feed my voracious caterpillar charges.

The monarchs grew from tiny eggs to fat green caterpillars the size of my ring finger in two weeks. Between the constant feeding and cleaning up their poop, it was like having a dozen obnoxious, gorgeous toddlers. I have never been so disgusted or awed as when the monarch caterpillars turned themselves into swaying J-shapes before going into their chrysalises, which is to say: stuffed themselves into small jade pots.

Until I got flushed by mushrooms.

WHAT I LOVED about the grow kit, besides the rapid growth, was all the shapes I could see in the oyster mushrooms as they emerged.

Because my goal in life, besides being a poetry cult recruiter, is to get people to know and love nature, I took pictures of the mushrooms every morning when I removed the plastic bag and misted the mushrooms.

I posted the pictures to Instagram and started playing a game of looking-like: one day they looked like trumpets and then the trunks of elephants. The next it was the sweep of vases and then the vulnerability of bared throats. I enjoyed this game, which was just me flexing my poet muscles, but also turning mushrooms into language.

When the first flush became beastly, almost overtaking the bag, the comments changed too. Instead of saying how beautiful the mushrooms were, the commentators seemed . . . uneasy.

My friend Perry, a writer cum arts administrator, wrote "THEY'RE TAKING OVER THE ROOM!" And then Yvonne chimed in, saying, "Are you not getting nervous? Won't they start moving on their own and swallow you all?"

Yvonne DM'd me.

"I have to say that I don't like the look of the mushrooms you are growing and I don't want them growing in my camper," she said. "What I wonder most is: how did they get there?"

It's strange to me that one of the things that I love most about mushrooms in forests – that they appear overnight and are gone the next day – is what most alarms other people.

WE COULDN'T NOT watch *The Last of Us* when it came out in January 2023. It was somehow everywhere, like airborne fungal spores/pollen/dirt/seeds.

Like *Hannibal*, *The Last of Us* had amazing special effects and a storyline that had been thoroughly tested in other formats. Hannibal Lecter had already had several outings in books and movies

– the most popular of which is 1991's *The Silence of the Lambs* –
while *The Last of Us* had its start as a popular video game launched
in 2013.

I liked how *The Last of Us* posited fungi as monsters, which I
thought wouldn't be a big leap for Yvonne and her ilk, who already
thought fungi were freaky. But as someone who had spent their
life watching Dutch elm disease – caused by *Ophiostoma ulmi*, an
ascomycete microfungus that infests the tree's vascular system –
slowly weaken and kill elm trees, I was probably more willing to
go along with the premise of the show than most.

The premise of *The Last of Us* is based on the idea that cordyceps fungi – that famously infest ants, taking control of their
circulatory system and thereby turning them into "zombie ants"
that march to spots on trees most suitable for fungal dispersal –
could/would infest humans. There are apparently more than four
hundred different species of cordyceps that use this strategy, each
specializing in a different insect, including wasps, moths and
grasshoppers.

It's not much of a leap from zombie ant to zombie human, from
documentary to TV show. Interestingly, the show also says that
climate change has made this leap to humans possible. In a scene
at the beginning of the show, scientists are being interviewed on
a 1960s TV program about potential pandemic viruses. Dr. Neuman says that viruses don't really worry him: "Viruses can make
us ill but fungi can alter our very minds," he says.

Neuman's pronouncement is greeted with disbelief, even
laughter from everyone: the other scientist, the host and the stu-
dio audience. But Dr. Neuman persists:

> True, fungi cannot survive if its host's internal temperature
> is over 94 degrees. Currently, there are no reasons for fungi
> to evolve to withstand higher temperatures. But what if that

were to change? What if, for instance, the world were to get slightly warmer? Now there *is* reason to evolve. One gene mutates . . . and any one of them could become capable of burrowing into our brains and taking control not of millions of us but billions of us. Billions of puppets with poisoned minds permanently fixed on one unifying goal: to spread the infection to every last human alive by any means necessary.

And then the show takes us into the near future, to a post-fungal epidemic where a greatly reduced population of humans have figured out ways to avoid if not eliminate coming into contact with the Infected, as the mushroom-controlled people are called, mostly by barricading themselves into the few remaining cities. Of course, *The Last of Us*'s zombies look like Eldon Stammets's victims had somehow gotten up and started attacking people. My favourite parts of the show were the mushroom-headed zombies, The Infected, created by UK makeup artist Barrie Gower. They're meant, of course, to evoke the cordyceps-fruiting bodies that emerge from the heads of the zombie ants, when they're high up on a branch and are stuck there with literal death grips. The real-life cordyceps-fruiting bodies are small and simple, with a cap and gills, compared to the fancy mushrooms that play them on TV. Those look like a mix between oyster mushrooms and chicken of the woods and completely obliterate everything from the lips up.

I also loved the way that hordes of the mushroom zombies could communicate via a mycelial network, so that the Infected all knew what one knew. It reminded me a little of the Borg, which are a race of cyborgs linked via a hive mind called "The Collective" in *Star Trek*.

But ultimately, the cordyceps-infested humans are just a zombie variant in a long line of zombie variants. The global fungal infection is ultimately incidental, in *The Last of Us*, to the human efforts to survive.

IF YOU HAVE to die.

If you have to die and be buried, a recent trend in the death care industry is natural burials, where people are not embalmed or buried in caskets but wrapped in shrouds and interred in shallow graves in park-like settings.

And if you're interested in a natural burial but don't want to pollute the land with the strange suitcase of chemicals that humans pack up over the course of our lives, you can buy a mushroom shroud or a suit infused with mycelia, though the science behind these suits has been called into question. You can even buy a coffin made of moulded mushroom mycelia for about $1,800 USD, the same material that IKEA and Dell are planning to use to replace Styrofoam in their packaging.

Basically, you can turn your dead body into a human/mushroom grow kit. And you don't even have to be a serial killer or a zombie to do it.

I saw my father's body at the funeral home just before he was cremated, waiting in a particleboard box. It was startling, mostly because his lips and nose looked like a melted candle or a mushroom instead of living skin.

I'd never seen a dead person up close before. I wanted to take a picture, so I could examine it later, privately, so I could remember it more firmly, but my youngest sister scowled at me.

There were Sharpies around his box so that we could write final messages on the particleboard that would be burned minutes later. I didn't write anything. I didn't touch what was left of him.

When I got back to the car, I looked in the rear-view mirror and saw my dad's nose on my face, suffused with blood. Living.

WHEN SPRING 2021 rolled around and Covid-19 restrictions eased, I took my used-up mushroom kit to my front garden, which would be just big enough for two bodies, if I were Eldon Stammets.

During the first and second world wars, governments advocated that people cultivate what they called Victory Gardens, to supplement the rations they were allotted but also to give people an activity that allowed them to remember the living world and so boost morale.

Many people turned to gardening during the two years of the pandemic, but my front yard is too shady for a proper veg garden, so I have a Neglect Garden, full of ferns and hostas.

My one concession to all the new activity in my neighbourhood and in distant friends' gardens, viewed via their social media, was to put in a new layer of mulch, hoping that it would retain moisture and keep down the weeds. And it mostly seemed to work, except in the driest of that summer's drought, where everything started to look a bit crispy.

I cut off the grow kit's knife-scarred plastic and set the sawdust block down on a bare patch in the garden. Over the summer, I mostly ignored it, noting how the outer crust of white mycelia fell away, leaving a rapidly disintegrating sawdust mass, as I walked to and from my car, to and from the recycle bin. It was like a tumour, slowly being reduced in size by a course of chemo/radiation. It was like an apple being nibbled away to nothing by a determined mouse.

Twice now, I have been surprised by a small flush of oyster mushrooms from my garden.

I have never felt so in love with the world as when I stood in my yard with a handful of mushrooms in one hand and watched my masked neighbours walk by, laughing and talking, in fall's golden light.

In the Kitschen

I WAS VISITING Tom Nagy's mushroom incubator/one-bedroom apartment. It was June 2022 and I was there to collect spent mushroom grow kits for my CSA garden, where I was hoping to grow mushrooms instead of – or in addition to – vegetables.

Tom's slogan as proprietor of River City Mushrooms is "cultivating mycological literacy." In addition to making and selling mushroom grow kits, he has given a variety of mushroomy talks and workshops around Winnipeg since moving here in 2015.

I looked around his apartment. I saw that he had gotten Adagio Acres' winter grain bundle and went, "of course." The bundle – really a small collection of paper sacks – produced by the Clarkleigh, MB–based farm is "a collection of grains, seeds, oils, flours and pulses grown on organic farms around the province, and processed/milled either by us, or the farmer growing the crop (if they have the processing/cleaning capacity on farm) to minimize the carbon footprint of transportation." The description explained that some of the products in the bundle would have become "on-farm food waste (downgraded to animal feed or composted) because of being a smaller quantity, or because of a lack of processing available here in the province." A few other friends of mine had ordered the bundle, but they were all serious bakers. I don't really understand baking: my oeuvre begins and ends with apple crisp. And sometimes rhubarb crisp.

I saw the home brewing, preserving and fermenting paraphernalia and went, "of course." Tom's day job is at Little Brown Jug, a craft brewery based in Winnipeg, so it makes sense that he'd also brew beer at home. But even if he'd had a completely different job, I still would have expected to see brewing gear in his apartment.

But as Tom gave me the tour, a part of me couldn't stop counting the number of mushroom decorations in his spic-and-span, impeccably organized apartment. This is, of course, in addition to all the mushroom-producing equipment and supplies, which also took up space. Standing in his kitchen, I asked Tom about his funginalia, his mushroom decorations, suggesting that people in his life had gotten them for him as gifts, knowing his love of mushrooms. Because that's how it had happened with me.

People are always so relieved when you announce that you have a "thing." Mention once you like turtles and then for five years, you're the recipient of turtle figurines of every make and model, size and shape.

Tom nodded, his eyes moving around his apartment.

"I haven't bought very many mushroom knickknacks," I told him, with a generous smear of smug on the toast of my statement. "I like mushrooms, not mushroom decorations."

At the door, I told him we should have a Zoom-based Mushroom Kitsch-off, where we'd announce a category – T-shirts!

Knickknacks! Posters! Mugs! – and then we'd have to hold our version of the "thing" up to the camera.

We laughed at this idea, then said our goodbyes.

Since then, I've realized that I am a dirty liar, that my home and person have slowly been infested with mushroom kitsch. Some of which I bought on purpose.

Ornaments / Stuffies

My mailbox has long been a source of mushrooms.

In December 2011, an unlabelled box appeared in my mailbox along with the weekend paper. It was a glass Xmas ornament of the old-timey variety, where you clip the ornament to the branches instead of hanging them. This was the same mechanism that was used to add real candles to Xmas trees back in the day, which I imagine was lovely. I just can't help thinking of how Xmas trees slowly dry out over the course of the holidays, becoming more and more flammable, and the nearby curtains, should the tree tip over . . .

Of course, the ornament was an *Amanita muscaria*, with red/orange glass tapering down to a white glass volva. But instead of white spots, it had silver spots painted on the glass. My response, when posting it to my social media: "Poison! Ornaments! Squeee!"

In November 2019, there was another unlabelled package in the mailbox, this time a rolled-up brown paper bag. When I opened it, it looked sort of suspicious, like someone had put something dead/furry in my mailbox. So instead of putting my hand in and grabbing it, I cut the bag away from the fur with scissors. I was tickled when I saw that it was a stuffie that resembled a shaggy mane or *Coprinus comatus*. Which is to say that it had a beige fun-fur cap mimicking what Michael Kuo describes as "large shaggy scales" on its cap, two black button eyes and a white corduroy stem with delicate white threads on the base, mimicking mycelial threads.

This being Winnipeg, I knew the stuffie maker Kami Goertz. We'd even worked together for a few years at Aqua Books, a used bookstore/performance space/restaurant, where she'd been the sous-chef and I'd been the event coordinator. At the time, I was about to launch my first book of poetry – on pregnancy, mothering and urban nature – and she was making stuffies and felted animals. (We bought a cat stuffie for Anna and she made me a tiny felted rabbit in a glass jar when she got my name for the staff Secret Santa. It was a rabbit terrarium!) Since then, we'd both become mushroom-obsessed. She regularly chimed in on the Winnipeg Mycological Society/Société mycologique de Winnipeg Facebook group, and she'd made a whole line of mushroom stuffies.

In November 2022, Kami and I did a version of my proposed Mushroom Kitsch-off contest with Tom. Except with Kami it was that I named a favourite mushroom and Kami shared a photo of her stuffie version on Instagram's messaging system. My favourite was her mushroom-adjacent ghost pipe or *Monotropa uniflora*, which doesn't have chlorophyll and has a parasitic relationship with a fungus that is in a mycorrhizal relationship with a tree.

In the case of the anonymous mailbox mushrooms, nearly a decade apart, I had my suspicions and I was right: they were from the writer Kerry Ryan, who lives down the street from me.

In April 2021, after we'd walked the Wolseley/Wellington loop together and I was feeling sentimental, I posted, "It's been nearly 30 years since we met in Catherine Hunter's creative writing class at the University of Winnipeg and she's been the best writer-friend I can imagine: talented, kind, generous, dryly funny."

"What would I do without you, Ariel?" Kerry replied. "Seriously, I'm not even sure if I'd still be writing now."

"Of course you would!" I answered. "Also: sniffle!"

Later, it occurred to me that Kerry's statement could be read in two ways.

"Also: are you blaming me?" I added to the post.

Kerry's reply was swift and brutal: "Only some days!"

Memes

Karen Dudley is my mushroom meme pusher.

Karen has written two mystery series in her long and varied career. The first featured Robyn Devara, a field biologist/detective and touched on issues around endangered species of birds and environmental degradation. The titles were perfection, in my opinion: *Hoot to Kill, The Red Heron, Macaws of Death* and *Ptarmaggedon*. Her second series was called the Epikurean Epic. It was set in the Roman era and her detective had a fascinating backstory: "Pelops' troubles began when his father chopped him into stewing meat and served him to the gods for tea. Although he's been remade, and gifted with a talent for the culinary arts, there are downsides – namely a missing shoulder and sea god with an infatuation." My favourite thing about *Food for the Gods* and the sequel, *Kraken Bake,* were the period details, which included the fact that breadsticks were often used as dildos by Greek matrons. (Ahem.)

So it should come as no surprise that in the time I have known Karen, I have often been summoned from writing time, from things I should be doing, by her tags on richly weird and wonderful tree and mushroom items.

In July 2020, she tagged me in a post with a photo montage that showed a pink-and-black-mottled thing emerging from a gelatinous egg. It looks like a nightmare hand, something that will drag you down into whatever hell you believe in. The text was as follows: "A fungus, *Clathrus archeri*, called Devil's Fingers or

Octopus Stinkhorn. The young fungus erupts from a suberumpent egg by forming into four to seven elongated slender arms initially erect and attached at the top. The arms then unfold to reveal a pinkish-red interior covered with a dark-olive spore-containing gleba. In maturity it smells like putrid flesh." ("Suberumpent," according to Michael Kuo, means "bursting through the surface of the substratum" and gleba is "the stinky, sticky, usually-olive-or-brown, spore-filled slime that covers some surface or surfaces on the stinkhorn to attract insects for spore dispersal.")

In real life I've only ever seen the common stinkhorn, which has a beige stem and a brown cap covered in putrid rotting-flesh-smelling ooze. Its Latin name is *Phallus impudicus*, meaning "shameless penis" and that seems terrible/appropriate because, of all the mushrooms I find, it's the one that most looks like a human penis. There's another stinkhorn named the *Mutinus caninus* or dog penis stinkhorn. I don't want to think about dog penises while walking in the woods! But it's a great and vulgar family of fungi. And Karen somehow knew . . .

In June 2021, she shared a meme with a photo of a sulking Pingu, which is to say the plasticine penguin character invented by Swiss animators Otmar Gutmann and Harald Muecke. Like Mr. Bean, Pingu communicates via a series of grunts and yelps. In the image, Pingu is sitting on a chair that is too big for him and his arms are crossed. The caption reads, "When you're at the family reunion and nobody wants to talk about trees and their mycorrhizal symbiotic interrelationships with fungi."

In April 2022, she tagged me in another Lighter Side of Science post, this one a link to an article from IFLScience.com entitled "Mushrooms May 'Talk' to Each Other And Have Vocabulary of 50 'Words.'"

On October 12, it was a meme that read, "I made a risotto with mushrooms I foraged locally. Not only was it delicious but a Welsh choir of purple elephants sang the whole *Bat Out of Hell* album accompanied by a light show." In the background, almost completely obscured by the white text, is a still life of food in dark tones. This brings me back to the various mushroom Facebook groups, where half the questions are "Is this a magic mushroom?" and the others are "Is this poisonous?"

Other memorable headlines include "Scientists Revive 32,000-Year-Old Plant Right Out of the Pleistocene" from a website called EarthlyMission.com and "Underground World of Fungi to Be Mapped for the First Time" from EcoWatch.com.

But in October 2019, Karen gifted me one of Kami Goertz's stuffies, the Blinky Cap mushroom, Kami's punny take on the inky cap or *Coprinopsis atramentaria*. Like the shaggy mane, the gills in inky caps "deliquesce," which means that they turn into black goo that is sometimes used as ink. Kami's Blinky Cap had a black felted cap with a single eye sewn into the middle and black strings hanging from the edges. It had the same beige corduroy stem and white thread mycelium.

So when Kerry's Shaggy Mane appeared in my mailbox, I thought it was a second gift from Karen and wondered if she expected my firstborn in exchange, like in most fairy tales.

Earrings

Not only do I own two pairs of mushroom earrings, I *commissioned* them!

One day, I was shopping in Annie's Attic, the cat café/thrift store operated by D'Arcy's ARC, the rescue where we got Kitty and Philip. I noticed that there was a display of handmade earrings at the till, made by a volunteer who went by Freckled Pearl as a fundraiser.

There were earrings made of resin clay, flattened and imprinted with various textures, and beaded earrings. Though none of the ones in the display appealed to me, I checked out her Instagram and really enjoyed her jewellery as well as her presence in my feed.

Her profile bio says that her name is Hillary Pearl, but the majority of our relationship has occurred online, so I think of her as Freckled Pearl. It also says that she is Red River Métis/Italian/Irish and that her earrings "may also contain cat fur."

I have no idea what Freckled Pearl looks like because she doesn't selfie, but she is a warm and cheerful presence in my feed, like light through my windows, and I trust her. So in May 2021 I messaged her on Instagram: "Hi! Could you make some mushroom earrings for me? I don't care if they're resin or beads!"

She responded almost right away, saying, "I could certainly try. Love mushrooms. Let me play around this week. Thanks for the inspiration, I've been a little dry."

My only condition for the earrings was not "red" mushrooms, by which I meant *Amanita muscarias*. My colour preference would be brown or orange, which are the colours, besides white and beige, of the mushrooms I find most often.

Pearl confided that she has five cats and three dogs, all from D'Arcy's ARC, in addition to her two children. And given the pandemic, she was homeschooling her children. We traded pictures of our cats. I sent pictures of Kitty and Philip, whom she remembered as Petra and Jacobi from her time as a volunteer with the rescue.

Pearl also mentioned that her partner was learning about mushrooms and trying to identify them.

Within two weeks, she sent pictures of red-and-brown beaded mushrooms, mentioning that she didn't have any orange beads. She added that she had also made clay ones.

"They were so fun to make once I figured it out," she commented.

"I'm glad I asked you to make them for me, then . . ." I responded.

The clay earrings were flat and the size of a loonie, with white stems and caps that were a mix of brown and golds. Beautiful. I decided to buy a pair of each kind, saying how lovely they were but also, "I'm greedy for mushrooms in whatever form!"

After some talk about price and the logistics of pickup, we returned to process-talk, which is honestly my favourite kind of talk.

"I've been feeling a little worn out with, you know – the world – and I haven't felt like creating but this gave me a nice push," she said.

"Yes, I've felt the same," I replied. "Just low/listless."

In September 2021, when a wet fall meant a flush of mushrooms in Assiniboine Forest, I sent her three photos.

"Hey! I thought I'd let you know that there are lots of orange amanitas in Assiniboine Forest right now, since you're making red amanita earrings."

"Oh myyyyy those are so beautiful," she answered.

"I thought you'd like them! (Toxic and also hallucinogenic . . .)"

It felt like the real end of the transaction: money for labour, real mushrooms for mushroom decorations.

Dishes

My mushroom kitsch pusher's name is Gwendolyn Funk.

I met Gwendolyn across a backyard bonfire at a friend's house. She likes all my posts about mushrooms and mudlarking, stained glass and public poetry projects, and slides into my DMs with links to mushroom kitsch.

In mid-December 2021, she'd sent a link to "Vintage geo z Lefton 1970 ceramic divided mushroom dish," a 6" x 12" platter for sale on Facebook Marketplace. It was twenty dollars and the seller was in what they described as "old St. Vital." My mother and sister had each lived nearby at different points, so I was familiar with the area. And so that's how I found myself in her backyard in the winter darkness, getting the platter from the designated drop-off box.

I wrote Gwendolyn to thank her for the tip.

"Ha! Fantastic. I guess I've clicked on enough mushroom things that they're just being offered up to me randomly now," she responded.

Over the months that followed, Gwendolyn sent me other things, but I didn't bite, commenting, "I am a reluctant purchaser of mushroom kitsch. Though I recently got two mushroom T-shirts from Redbubble."

The mushroom T-shirt purchase seems to have spurred her on.

On October 7, she sent me "Vintage Mushroom Cream & Sugar Set," which was selling for twenty-five dollars. They were horrible but also appealing, the main body of both being beige and textured with lines that were supposed to look like wood, I think, with clusters of mushrooms with light-brown caps and beige stems on the sides of each piece. The sugar bowl had yellow-capped mushrooms as handles and the top was supposed to be a mushroom cap but also had a yellow knob on it.

I clicked through and found that the seller also had "Vintage Ceramic Mushroom Set," which had eight pieces. Most importantly – given my thrifty Winnipegger background – it was on sale, marked down to fifty dollars from one hundred. My consumer brain nattered, "Get this one! Four times as many pieces for only twice the price!" But no! I didn't need it!

The seller had written the following no-nonsense text to go with her well-lit photos: "Selling as a lot only. Includes gravy boat with plate, teapot, salt and pepper shakers, cream and sugar bowl, and a napkin holder. The napkin holder has some minor chips on the grass as shown on photo #9, but otherwise all pieces are in excellent condition! Pick-up in North Kildonan. For other vintage items and collectibles, see my other ads." The tags were "mushroom dishes," "mushroom canister" and "merry mushroom."

Later that afternoon, I posted to Facebook: "I waaaaaaant this, but I don't neeeeed this. Help talk me out of it, Oh Internets!!" My friends are terrible, so what they offered as 'help' was unwanted validation of my late-stage capitalism bad decisions. And mushroom puns.

My dim sum friend and communications genius Julie Kentner wrote, "You totally need it." Paula Jane Remlinger, a Saskatchewan poet, chimed in to say, "It won't take up mush room!" Fellow SK writer Andréa Ledding wrote, "Just in time for Thanksgiving! You can always be the FunGi at every gathering! do ittttttt." Then Gwendolyn got in the action, writing: "Sorry for always tempting you with potential mushroom rabbit holes! Or am I?" To which I responded, in all caps, that she didn't seem sorry, to which she responded "IT'S BECAUSE I KNOW SECRETLY YOU WANT THESE THINGS. Even if there's no room for all of them."

On October 9, I captioned a picture of a mushroom-themed tea set, pictured in a box on my lap in the car: "I am ashamed and sated."

Encouraged by my weakness, Gwendolyn sent "Vintage Wooden Mushroom & Bird Candlestick Holder" (ten dollars) on October 7, "Vintage 1978 ceramic mushroom mugs" (thirty-six dollars) on October 9 and "Double mushroom ring" (ten dollars) October 10. Sandy Pool also sent me the 1978 mugs on October 9, saying, "Not trying to ruin your lyfe or anything BUT . . ." And then November 16, she sent "Mushroom dish's ($50)," commenting, "Not to be an enabler buuuttt."

The seller described the listing as "Mushroom serving dish's Teapot Milk container And sugar container – sugar container is a separate pattern and material" but attempted to sweeten the deal by putting everything on an embroidered tablecloth. It was still listed at the end of November and I went so far as to message the seller, asking if it was still available. But I resisted.

Other friends started sending me ads for mushroom kitsch, which of course was added to the links and tags to mushroomy articles and artworks that circulate in cycles across my feeds.

It's interesting to see how many friends will tag me or message me about what I call "Internet Mushrooms," which seem to have a thriving mycelium network of their own.

T-Shirt

I only got those Redbubble T-shirts because I was abandoning my only child on her birthday. I was leaving town for a conference that fell on Anna's sixteenth birthday in June.

Her expectations on this matter were clear and were based on our experience of her eleventh birthday, when I had been sent to a publishing conference in Austin, Texas. Mike elected to come with me and so Anna went to stay with Mike's parents for the week, which included her birthday. Though she was with people she knew and loved, who knew and loved her, though we left presents, extra presents, and called the day before and on the day, she still really *really* missed us.

But, after much negotiation, we had a plan. We'd pull her from school on the day of her birthday and she and I would spend the morning and most of the afternoon together before I left for the airport. We'd have her birthday supper the night before, including ice cream cake from her favourite artisanal ice cream store.

My writer-friend and co-conspirator Tanis MacDonald, whose book *Straggle: Adventures in Walking While Female* would be launched at the conference, wanted to get Anna a "thanks for letting us steal your mother away" present. I suggested Redbubble, a website that sells stickers and T-shirts and tote bags from user-supplied artwork, similar to Society6. Anna had gotten fan-art stickers for her favourite characters from TV shows and movies from the site, so I knew she could use a gift certificate. But after Tanis registered for a Redbubble account and bought a gift card for Anna, the site gave Tanis an additional credit she could send to someone.

So she sent it to me, writing: "P.S. There are lots of mushroom things."

I looked and *oh my yes* there were. So I used the credit to buy a grey T-shirt with a big white spore print and an olive-green shirt with a vintage mushroom poster. I also got some mushroom stickers, including one where a naked lower body emerged from a mushroom cap and another with clusters of a few different mushrooms and ferns.

Anna looked over my stickers when they arrived. She pointed to one that had two hands holding a handful of forest that included soil, greenery, mushrooms and a small, calm-looking toad, rendered in a palette of pink, magenta and orange.

"Those are lesbian flag colours," she noted. "Sometimes closet lesbians whose parents are conservative will get stickers in the flag colours and put them up as a way of being visible but safe."

I have never heard of mushroom kitsch being better deployed than that.

Sweater

In September I showed up at Tom's house on some mushroomy business.

I was wearing my new sweater from ModCloth, called "So Mushroom in My Heart V-Neck Sweater," even though it was a bit too warm for the day.

"What is *that*?" Tom asked when he came to the door, his mushroom cut bobbing in the sunlight, his lips twisted with the slightest derision.

I'd bought the sweater in November 2021 as a Black Friday impulse (40 percent off) and promptly posted about it to social media: "I got a mushroom sweater. IT IS RESEARCH FOR MY BOOK." My friend Tessa, who can quilt and garden and run wire for your newsroom, said, "Research my ass. Admit it was awesome and you wanted it." My Icelandic/Ukrainian friend Amy Stefanson, who taught me to make vinarterta, that Icelandic diasporic dessert, whose Ukrainian grandmother kept foraging for mushrooms after immigrating to Saskatchewan as a young woman, said: "Important and fashionable research!!! I have had mushroom socks in a shopping tab for weeks now. Should probably just purchase . . ."

Most importantly, my publisher Noelle said, "Why should you resist something so perfect?"

At the time, I'd thought, "Why indeed?" and stuffed it into the woolly section of my closet.

But this was the first time I'd worn it out in public. If I'd been at a support group, I would have declared, "My name is Ariel Gordon and I may . . . have a bit . . . of a . . . problem . . . with mushroom kitsch!"

But this was a sunlit apartment of someone who'd let mushrooms kick him out of his bedroom. So instead, I looked Tom in the eyes, smiled big and shrugged.

Morel Hunter

I HAVE ALWAYS wanted to find mushroom kindred spirits and the Winnipeg Mycological Society/Société mycologique de Winnipeg group on Facebook had them in every shape and size, from newbies dumping a hatful of random mushrooms to experts sharing a table full of morels. The group currently has 4,800 members and is led by Alexandre Brassard, the Dean of Arts and Science at the Université de Saint-Boniface and a political scientist by training.

The threshold for membership is gloriously low: "Intrigued by mushrooms? This is a forum to learn more about them and to talk about the fungi of Manitoba and the Canadian Prairies. This Facebook page is the ideal place to discuss Prairie species and sites, to share foraging and cultivation tips, to support the correct identification of local mushrooms, and to share news about mycological events in Winnipeg."

Serious mushrooming is often about research. What trees are in association with the mushrooms you're after? What kind of soil/ moisture level do they prefer? Do they flush the year after forest fires? Where were the most recent forest fires? What Crown land (or property owned by a friend) meet all of these criteria? I have done the bulk of my mushrooming in a few spots. I've become a specialist of mushrooms in aspen/oak parkland, but, more specifically, in Assiniboine Forest. I'm not good at mushrooms in coniferous forests or even mixed deciduous forests.

I'd only ever found a handful of morels, in one spot on the Harte Trail in Assiniboine Forest and then another handful in the Belair Forest. But the group had lots of people finding morels or talking about finding morels, with tips on where/when to find them.

People are secretive about their "spots," the locations on Crown land that produce the mushrooms they're looking for in profusion, year over year. But enough people had let slip that poplar forests in Southeastern Manitoba, and specifically in Sandilands Provincial Forest, were good sites.

So Mike and I got up early on a Saturday and drove out. Given that Sandilands is a big place, I did some searching and discovered that the Sandilands Ski Club had two parking lots, one of which was described as being hillier. So we headed toward that one, using the GPS tag from their website.

We parked and set out on one of their cleared ski trails, which had long since melted. And of course the trees were wrong: conifers and birches. We kept walking, scanning the horizon for white/ grey trunks. One whole section was completely swamped with water, where we had to walk from shoal to shoal or just try to avoid the bigger pools.

Of course, that's also where all the non-morel mushrooms

were. Mike spotted devil's urn (*Urnula craterium*), a black mushroom that's the shape of a cauldron. I'd never seen it before, but people had been posting it to the WMS, alongside a similar looking species, witches' cauldron (*Sarcosoma globosum*), which is brown instead of black. I spotted three types of jelly fungi, including blobs of yellow witches' butter, a brown variety and a black variety that completely covered sections of trunk on young trees. There were also mushrooms on stumps and downed trees.

Another pleasure, while walking through higher sandy areas, were all the prairie crocuses. One of my spring requirements is finding and photographing prairie crocuses while they're blooming. Before two years ago, I hadn't seen them very often, even though they're the provincial flower. I think it's because the areas I regularly walk in aren't prime territory for them – like morels, they like sand. Previously, I'd go find them in Little Mountain Park, a city park that is mostly an off-leash dog park. I'd wait until a friend who took her dog there regularly posted about them. But we'd had good luck finding at least one prairie crocus the last two years and one was all I needed.

This year, I had heard that they were blooming, but I hadn't had the chance to head to LMP yet. There were some blooming in the native prairie garden in the Wolseley Community Gardens' Vimy Ridge Garden, and I was there anyway, helping to shovel mulch into the beds, so I took a photo of them. But they were a placeholder for me until I could find something in the wild. "Someone came and dug one of the crocuses out," one of the garden organizers said, surveying the bed. She shrugged: that kind of activity was part of what happened in community gardens. And at least whoever it was hadn't taken every plant. But prairie crocuses were everywhere in Sandilands, even by the side of the road. They became common, so I eventually only stopped for large clusters of them.

We trudged through the swamped area, skipped through the crocus area and eventually found an area that was mostly poplars. We walked through that for twenty minutes before we found our first mushroom.

We found one, and then a handful, and then a bagful, moving slowly, trying to look sideways. We would often call out to each other: "There's one by your foot. And another and oh, look, another." I got out my mushroom knife, given to me at Xmas, and was using it to cut the stems, though they were delicate and often snapped between our fingers. I also used my knife to collect a handful of fiddleheads, the early coiled leaves of ostrich ferns, which were also coming up in that area.

I knew that these were early spring morels, *Verpa bohemica*. But verpas are in the Morchellaceae family with the more standard *M. angusticeps* and so should just be called morels. I'd seen verpas on the WMS group. Unlike true morels, which were empty inside, verpas had a cotton candy–like fuzz inside their stems and caps. Also, they were much taller than true morels, and the texture of the cap was different.

We also found two small black morels. All in all, we felt very successful as we walked back to the car.

THERE IS SOME debate on WMS and in the broader community as to whether verpas are edible, but I decided to try them.

I found a recipe on a website called Cooking to Entertain for verpas in a shallot vermouth sauce, but was mostly reading for the cooking instructions: "To begin the preparation fill a bowl with lightly salted cold water. Add the *Verpa bohemica* mushrooms and give a shake. After fifteen minutes pour out the water and refill the bowl with more cold water. Do this three times. After the third time, lay your morels out on some paper towel and pat dry." I'd read elsewhere that they should be parboiled or even just boiled twice. But I elected to use this method: given how delicate they were, I was worried that they'd fall apart if they were boiled. Even the soaking process disconnected most of the caps from the stems. I spent two hours soaking and draining my mushrooms, which had already started to soften in the mesh bag I'd collected them in.

I made a soup with the caps and some of the stems, with store-bought pho-flavoured broth, adding onions, garlic and cilantro. When it was done, Mike and I each had a spoonful, as is recommended with all new foods but specifically wild mushrooms, and also wild mushrooms that are sort of questionable.

The next day, neither of us had any aches and pains that were out of the ordinary for middle-aged people. We should have been fine to have big bowls of soup, which had looked and smelled delicious, but we left it in the fridge instead. Part of our hesitation was that our fridge was full of other options, but part of it was fear. The soup was in the bottom of the fridge, waiting. And food waste was one of my least favourite things. Was I going to let my fear win? Or was I going to wait until it went bad and throw it out? Finally, two days later, I reheated a bowl, adding some shredded pork that had been cooked carnitas style. And it was delicious. Mushroomy but not overly so. It was meaty and not just because I'd added the pork. My soups are not always great: I'm much better at making meatballs and stir-fries for some reason. But this was probably the best soup I'd ever made.

I made a point of telling Mike how good it was. But he said he wasn't sure if it was worth it, given the potential side effects. I experienced no side effects. So the next day, I had another bowl. I felt sustained by the soup, by the idea that I'd collected the mushrooms and had carefully prepared them, but also because I'd overcome my fear. There was one bowlful left. Mike still hadn't had any, but he's not as passionate about mushrooms as I am. And I had to respect his wariness.

But if the pandemic had taught me anything, it's that we're always assuming risk.

FOUR DAYS LATER, I drove out to Sandilands again. This time, I was alone. I had been waffling about going, feeling like I should write but knowing that this was the only day I had free this week. Otherwise, I'd have to wait until Sunday and the morels might be finished by then.

So I posted to FB, which is what I do when I want to justify my bad decisions: "To write about mushrooms or go looking for them, morel season in full flush?"

Noelle Allen, my publisher, was the first to chime in: "Go looking! Write later."

And that was all I needed. I grabbed my new-to-me mushrooming bag, a pleather bowling bag in deep brown, and started assembling my supplies: my new mushrooming knife, a cloth shopping bag to put morels in and a snack. I also needed to refill my water bottle and make tea in my travel mug.

We dropped Anna off at school and then drove to Mike's parents' house, where he would spend the rest of the week building a deck for them. Just before I got back in the car, Mike said, "My light rain jacket is in the back . . . I think it's supposed to rain."

"Okay," I said, then got in the car and started driving toward Sandilands.

On the way, I noticed a sign that noted that a stretch of highway was available for adoption. I had the vague sense that it meant that a local community group was responsible for coming and picking up garbage semi-periodically, but I thought it was funny. Do you adopt a highway because you hope it'll grow up and become a path in the woods or a freeway? Can a highway be a dependent, the way other things you can adopt – human children and species we've decided are pets – are dependents? I know we're mired in late-capitalism car culture, like in a mud puddle or a moat of oil, but do highways really count as dependents? There were also several stretches of the one hundred kilometres of highway that were under construction, including one or two with "Speed Fines Double" and "Max 60 km Per Hour in a Construction Zone" though I saw no construction workers, machines or obvious roadworks.

I arrived, parked in the same spot as before and immediately set out for the stretch of woods that I knew was mostly poplars, though instead of walking next to the highway for the first bit, I walked in the woods, which meant that I had to adjust my course several times. Of course, I got hot right away and removed the cardigan. Immediately, a huge mosquito, the first I'd seen this spring, landed on my arm. But mostly, I didn't notice the bugs, given that I was crashing through the bush.

It took me half an hour to walk to the zone that was mostly poplars, with boggy areas and slopes. Along the way, I noticed that the buds on the marsh marigolds we'd found on the weekend were open. I also saw small clumps of wild violets.

"Check and check," I thought to myself. Those are some of the things that WMS members had listed as signs that morels were likely present.

And then I found one morel. It was low to the ground and dark, unlike the verpas we'd found last week, which were tall with beige-y stems and a faintly wrinkled brown to warm grey cap. I immediately stopped and looked around. And there was another one, a step behind me. And then I spotted five or six more, in the underbrush within ten feet of the first one.

"If you see one morel, look around. There's probably more." was another piece of advice in the WMS.

But looking for morels is really a hunt. Usually, if you're in an area with the right conditions for a particular mushroom, they'll be there in profusion. I'm thinking about lobster mushrooms or puffballs or even devil's fingers. They're usually in clusters or colonies and very easy to see, once you've found the first one. Morels are different. I kept on finding and then losing them. It was like magic: they'd reveal themselves to me if I looked at them slant, if I looked at the undergrowth with my peripheral vision, but if I took a step or turned around, I'd lose them again. It was like they'd always been there when I found them. They were obvious, dark and honeycombed. Small and perfect, almost too beautiful to be real. And then they'd be gone.

After more than twenty years of mushrooming I am good at noticing the forest floor, at finding mushrooms, but this was a challenge. So I walked that one spot backward and forward, radiated out from the first morel, came back, tried again. I collected a handful of morels. And I thought, "Okay, now that I've found them, I'll find them everywhere."

But that wasn't true. I kept looking but wasn't seeing anything. After a while, I put the black shopping bag back in my bag and closed my mushrooming knife, mostly because I'm not used to handling a knife outside my kitchen and was worried I'd trip and fall on it or cut myself. Also, I was taking pictures of the other things you'd find in a spring forest: a deer jawbone, prairie crocuses, other mushrooms.

I spent forty minutes walking the length and breadth of this boggy stand of poplars, looking for a place fifteen feet up from the water, which was in the low spots. Looking for a hummock with moss, which I'd noticed in other people's photos.

By the time I found another morel, I almost didn't believe they existed. And then it was only another handful. And then: a single morel near a patch of verpas.

The weirdest patch was when I realized that I'd been walking for nearly three hours and was both famished and tired. I consulted my mapping app to see how near/far I was from the car and decided to walk the roadside path for part of the return trip, to minimize the time I'd spend crashing through the bush.

And there was a morel. And then another. And then a handful. *What was happening?* And then I looked. I could see a low wet spot surrounded by large poplars fifteen feet away. And this ditch-adjacent trail was higher, fringed by baby poplars. So it was right, in a way, but it still felt odd. I mean, why crash through the bush at all if you can just walk next to the highway?

As I made my way back to the car, I found several little streams and even a patch where I was surrounded by verpas. This was unusual, because I had found very few of them on the rest of my travels and the ones I did find were mature, even wizened. Sometimes, I'd just find the beige stem, the cap having fallen off or been bitten off by deer. I wasn't going to pick verpas. I was after morels today and I still had a soup with verpas in it I was faintly afraid of back at home. And then I reconsidered. At that point, I hadn't seen a morel in ages, so I picked one, thinking that I'd carry it along and take peeks at it to console myself. And then, pushing through a dense spot, the verpa was beheaded. *Oh well.*

I was taking wide quad trails and narrower cross-country ski trails to get back to the car when it started to rain. I pulled my sweater from around my waist but struggled to get into it. Fifty metres from the car, there was a tree that had fallen on the path. I had to step through it and there were several branches on the ground. I thought one of them might be a good air freshener for the car on the way home, so I picked it up. I also picked up all the roadside litter, which was mostly metal cans and plastic bottles. It is something I could do and by the time I was back at the car, my hands and the big pockets down the front of my jacket were full.

When I got to the car, I stowed the bough, emptied my trash pockets, then changed out my battered rainboots for my Blundstones. I had prepped a drive-home bag for my morels: a green Superstore bin lined with a tea towel. It sat on the passenger seat of the car, waiting.

The rain had started to pelt down when I finally opened the driver's-side door and swung into my seat.

I opened the mushroom bag, the "perfect" bag whose strap had rubbed my neck all day, and it was empty. No cloth bag. Just my water bottle.

I heaved myself out of the car and opened the passenger side doors one after another. Where was it? With my shoes? No. In the front seat footwell with my regular bag? No? Was it under the conifer bough, somehow? No.

It was back on the trail. I could remember the last morel I picked, in a spot where I was surrounded by verpas. But I was so careful about putting the cloth bag back in my mushrooming bag and even zipping it closed. Except I'd been pushing my way between dense brush. Except after finding the last morel I was tired and hungry and had a long walk back to the car, so maybe I hadn't zipped it closed the last time. But I couldn't remember precisely the route I'd taken back. It was a hungry/tired blur.

I stood in the rain, thinking, close to tears. Was it possible that I'd spent three hours walking in the bush, each handful of morels representing an hour of walking, each handful of morels a spike of elation and then an hour where I wasn't sure they existed, where I wanted to take the bag out and look at the morels but kept swinging my eyes back and forth across the ground? I got back in the car. I could give up and go home with the mushroom pictures I had on my phone. What was that old saying? "Take nothing but photographs. Leave nothing but footprints."

But this was Crown land. I was allowed to pick mushrooms

(and fiddleheads) here. I had to try to find them. But I knew that I didn't need to re-walk that last kilometre. So I grabbed the apple I'd packed this morning, to take the edge off my hunger, and started the car. Biting big chunks out of the apple and furiously chewing them I backed out of the sandy pull-in that was the Sandilands Ski Club's main parking lot, and drove the five hundred metres to the quad road. I pulled in behind a truck and trailer combo and started walking, only remembering when I got to the flooded-out section that I'd changed out of my rainboots. But I got through. I saw the intersection with the garbage piled on it. And I turned right. Which looked familiar, as we'd walked that route the week before, but when I got to the view of the road with the signs pointing one way to Marchand and the other to Woodridge I was confused. This wasn't the route I'd taken today. I felt a sob rising in my throat. I should give up, go back to my car and drive home.

I got back to the garbage-heaped crossroads. I took a breath. And I turned the other way. This stretch of road had a slight slope. And I could see the pond on my right. Looking toward the trees on the other side of the road, I saw something black on the road.

"Oh please," I said, and picked up the pace.

And there, in the middle of quad tracks, in the sand, was my cloth bag. I noticed for the first time that it had the logo of the Manitoba Moose in gold on the black fabric. I opened it and looked down at my appearing/disappearing morels, the results of half a day of walking, of sustained attention to the ground. I walked more slowly back down the slope, through the flooded section and back to my car.

I very carefully laid them out on the tea towel in the green bin before swinging around on the sandy road and up onto the highway, rain coming down.

I had planned to drive to Steinbach for lunch again, but it was getting late and I knew I had to pick Mike up from his parents'. So

I grabbed the bag of veggies I'd also packed and had taken a few bites when I felt the telltale tickle of a tick scaling my neck.

I reached for it, squeezing the squirming red bug between my finger and thumb, and reached for the button that lowered the window. I was driving a hundred kilometres per hour on a wet road, trying to pay attention to the road, to the other cars, but I also wanted to get the tick out of the car. It was almost an instinctive response: *Get it out! Now!* It was the closest thing I had to fear of anything in the natural world. Not just for the creeping around, for the ways they hide on the body, becoming engorged with blood, but also how hard it had been, historically, to get diagnosis and treatment of Lyme disease in Canada.

I put my hand out a few inches and released the tick, hoping the onrushing wind wasn't blowing it back into the car. And so it went, the rest of the drive home. Ticks on my neck. Ticks on my shoulders and lower back. One time, I was looking in the rear-view mirror and saw a tick crawl out of my hair onto my ear. I threw a few into the footwell, aware that I was driving badly, that the ticks were adding to the bad decision-making that hunger and fatigue had already prompted: *Feeling famished, on the verge of hangry? Don't stop for food. Covered in ticks? Don't pull over and get them off you in a calm, deliberate manner.* Instead, all the way to Winnipeg, I opened my window and threw ticks out. Given how constant their appearance was, at one point I wondered if I was just blowing them back in and started sticking my arm out as far as it would reach. Between the pressure from the wind and the persistence of the rain, it felt like I was Thor, lifting my hammer into the storm I'd created. Except I was trying to lose ticks in the wind and rain. Except I hadn't deliberately called the ticks to me, except that I'd chosen to walk in the bush in spring. Except ticks weren't a weapon I could wield.

On the way back, which felt twice as long as the way out, I saw the Adopt-a-Highway signs again. And I realized that I had adopted a whole nest of ticks, given the range of sizes and the numbers. (I'm going to say twenty-five?) It was, by far, the most ticks I have ever had on me at one time. The previous record was nine, but usually I get three in high-tick areas. Most of the time, I find zero ticks on me.

I drove all the way to Mike's parents' house, only to discover that he'd texted me just after I'd left to say that I didn't need to come pick him up because he was going to pick up wood for the deck and would be a couple of hours yet. Of course, I hadn't seen the text and, by the time I got to their house, I didn't want to drive anymore. I had to drive across the city to our house, still scrabbling at ticks on my neck.

I dropped three out-of-town ticks on the road in Winnipeg.

When I finally got home, I grabbed a container of leftover cut-up fruit, another with veg and a container of hummus and took them upstairs to the washroom. I stood next to the shower and gobbled fruit, literally feeling sweet relief as the sugars in the fruit got into my system. Next, I stripped down, all my sweaty, dirty, rain-sodden, tick-ridden clothing in a damp pile on the floor. I practically leapt into the shower, hoping to wash away my discomfort and also the last of the ticks.

I found two ticks on me when I was lying on my bed in my towel, eating the rest of the fruit, dipping the veg in the hummus, which I'd balanced on my stomach. I marched back to the bathroom and flushed them. I found two ticks in the car the next day. By which I mean I found two ticks on me the next day, which logically had to have been ones that I threw on the footwell or that never made it to my poor neck.

Generally, walking in the woods would be considered a healthy activity. It is strange to think that illness could creep from the forest floor, the shrubs and grasses, onto your clothes and onto your skin. That you could never be same.

I ate every morsel of those three handfuls of morels, shrunk down in the pan but enough for topping two big pieces of seedy multigrain toast, dripping with margarine. One meal cost me seventy-seven dollars, or three and a half hours of my time at my non-profit rate of twenty-two dollars per hour.

It was so good, I called Anna down from her attic bedroom to take a bite of my mushroom toast, which I considered to be a great personal sacrifice. She tried it but wrinkled her nose. It was good, she said, but still a mushroom. *And I don't like mushrooms, Mummy.* My heart!

I taunted Mike with photos. He was across the city, building that deck at his parents', cross-hatchings of wooden planks, even as I'd spent the day crashing through winter constructions of twigs.

I also slurped down that last bowl of verpa soup, tasting my own fear but also garlic and the subtle umami of the mushrooms, layered with shredded pork.

It was Sunday at 8:00 a.m., a week later, and I'd decided I wanted to try somewhere new. Tom Nagy had mentioned that he often looked near the Ponds or the Pits, which was accessible from the highway near Ste. Anne.

By 9:00 a.m., Mike and I had looked at a map, trying to plot out a route. We weren't sure what was Crown land and what was private property in likely locations near Ste. Anne, so we found a set of ponds a little farther away, near Richer, that were accessible via a fire road.

Mike had spent much of the previous day putting the final screws in the deck at his parents' and said he felt too tired to come with me, so I set out by myself.

I was packing my mushrooming bag and filling my water bottle when I heard him read a headline, "Woman assaulted near Reynolds Ponds."

I stopped halfway to Ste. Anne at a Tim Hortons, realizing that it would probably be a good idea to have at least something that resembled a snack for later, besides the apple that I'd tucked into my bag. I got a whole wheat bagel with regular cream cheese. While I was there, Tom messaged me, asking where I had decided to go. I mentioned that I was heading to Ste. Anne and he replied that another likely spot is off Fire Road #13. Which was where I was heading, but I hadn't realized that yet.

I arrived at the spot that Mike and I had pinned on the map, which had a turnaround just off the road. For twenty minutes, a big truck and trailer had been in my rear-view mirror, and it was making me nervous. I'm not someone who is easily scared, but I'd just realized that I was alone in the middle of nowhere. The truck pulled to a stop next to me, the truck and trailer bearing logos of a construction company. Two young men and a dog were inside the cab. They rolled down their window and asked if I knew where the fish were. There were ponds on either side of us but I wasn't sure if they were natural ponds or gravel pits or if there were any fish in them.

"I'm here looking for mushrooms," I answered. "Which is an entirely different thing."

We both laughed and they kept driving. For whatever reason, I didn't want them to park next to me. I didn't want to chat with them again or have them watch me enter the woods. I waited until they were five hundred metres ahead of me before getting out of the car. I walked up the roundabout and realized that it was a hunters' spot, with dozens of red and blue empty shotgun shells on the ground. There were spots where deer had obviously been gutted, the ground covered with loose fur, and where there wasn't fur, there was garbage.

It didn't feel good, so I walked away from it as quickly as I could, entering the first stand of poplars I found. I crashed around for a while, looking at wildflowers, but it had been a hot and wet week and the mosquitoes had emerged. Every time I tried to stop and take pictures of the flowers or mushrooms on trees, they converged on my hands, my face and my legs, biting me through my tights.

I was frustrated and empty-handed. I returned to the car. Tom had texted to ask me how it was going, so I asked him to give me directions to the general area in St. Anne. He sent me a pinned location and, according to my mapping app, it wasn't far, so I drove farther down Fire Road #13.

I stopped at the edge of a stand of poplars that had been cut down, thinking that maybe the morels would still be there. I walked around, in and out of the right trees, then the wrong trees. I went back to the car and drove a bit farther, then stopped and plunged into the trees beside the road. There were other cars, all of which were full of men, noticing me as they went by. At one point, I hid in the trees so they wouldn't see me.

It had somehow been almost four hours. I was hungry and tired and decided to call it a day, so I checked my mapping app again. It told me that the main highway was only ten kilometres away if I kept going, but twenty-five if I went back the way I'd come. And I didn't want to go back the way I'd come because of all the men in cars.

The road got progressively worse, with washouts and ruts, but I was concentrating on what was in front of me instead of going, "The road is getting pretty bad. Maybe I should turn around after all."

And then I got to a section with a deep rut. But still I thought I could make it. And then I was stuck.

I had reconciled myself to no morels when I'd started driving. It was a hunt, after all, and I was the most inexperienced of hunters. But I did not expect to get myself stuck.

I walked short loops to and from the car, then the loops got bigger. In and out of shade and sun, a slight breeze somehow, and I trained my senses on what was around me to entertain myself. And then, five minutes before Mike arrived, when I was the farthest away from the car that I had been so far, I found morels. I had read about roadside morels covered in aspen fluff on the WMS and had been passively scanning the roadside. And then I spotted them – tall, thick, yellowy morels, but past their prime and coated with aspen fluff. Five of them in a ten-foot stretch, only two in a state I would eat, but I took them anyway.

I had them in my hand when Mike's car appeared at 3:00 p.m., when he came to a stop next to me.

I didn't even have time to say, "Look what I found!" before Mike spoke.

"Like driving on the moon," he sputtered. "What were you *doing*? Were you *trying* to break the car?"

"Let's just focus on getting out of here," I said, carefully, grateful that he was there, anticipating sitting in his cool car.

The hour after Mike arrived was awful. First, we collected fallen branches to put under the worst tire, the front passenger side wheel, the one that had sprayed mud all up the side of the car.

Mike stood next to the car, I drove, with the front passenger window halfway down so he could give me instructions. I put the car in reverse, turned the wheel this way and that, tiptoed on the gas pedal. The car didn't move. Then we rearranged the sticks, we dug at the hill of mud under the rear passenger wheel, trying to rectify the terrible differential between the tires. Then, when that didn't work, we put the floor mats under one tire and then both. Nothing.

Our hands were filthy, there were bugs all over us, the sun was hot and making us squint. One of the floor mats had been sucked under the car. I washed my muddy hands in the puddle that was filling one of the ruts my car wasn't in. The water was cloudy but most of the mud had sunk to the bottom and it was better than not washing my hands. Or using my drinking water to wash them. Mike was holding his hands up awkwardly, like he was holding a pair of filthy mittens that he would like to put down. I gestured toward another puddle. He shook his head no, then shrugged and did it.

We retreated to Mike's car. He started it and the blessed air conditioning washed over me. We killed all the mosquitoes in the car and then I called CAA.

It was such a goddamn relief to sit in Mike's cool car and drink the dregs of my tea and eat a granola bar. I never idle my car in the city but I was so grateful this time, having been too hot and too buggy for hours.

Mike found a container of wipes in his car and we washed the puddle water and the last of the mud off our hands. I was tired of this bit of the woods, the wet world full of mosquitoes.

Somehow, my phone could make calls and receive texts, but it seemed to take five minutes for each one to send. Mike's phone, on another cell phone carrier, couldn't make calls but texts zinged in and out. After phone calls to CAA and from the tow truck company in Steinbach, after trying and failing to send our location and then having to get Mike to send the location, we settled in to wait.

I'd left the city at 9:00 a.m. It was 5:33 p.m. and the tow truck hadn't arrived yet.

I AM NOT someone who has spent enormous amounts of time in the bush.

I have spent time in cottage country, where you have to drive and then boat to your cabin. Where there is a generator and thus electricity and even showers in the evenings. I have spent time in provincial parks, but in the lakeside campgrounds or cabins.

I was born and raised in the city by sort-of-nature-y people. They didn't take us on hikes or teach us how to fish, though my dad's siblings had convinced them to buy into a family cabin and they loved it in their own way. But I discovered the joys of nature on my own.

My uncle was a dedicated fisherman with a fishing boat and related gear he kept at the cabin. He was invested in teaching his two sons how to fish. When both families were at the cabin at the same time and he was giving his sons bedtime instructions about going fishing the next day, I would sometimes ask if I could go with them. My uncle would look irritated or sigh but to his credit he usually said something like, "If you get up on time on your own, you can come."

I loved to see his surprised face in the morning, when I slipped out of my bedroom, dressed and ready to go.

And I caught some fish, but mostly I liked being up early and the strange rituals of fishing. The round containers full of wriggling worms in the cooler or the yellow and white container that floated in the water with minnows. The drama of the bowed rods, someone getting the net for scooping the fish out of the water ready once the fish had been reeled close to the surface of the water.

My uncle made us fillet our own fish, which I enjoyed and feared at the same time: the strange insides of the fish, the ultra-sharp blade, not wanting to waste any of the meat. My uncle also hunted ducks and always had labs for prompt duck retrieval, but he never took me with him. I don't think my dad ever went with him, either . . .

WE WAITED IN the car, watching the CAA truck approach on their tracking app. It seemed to take longer than it should, but that could be put down to the fact that I'd spent five hours by the side of the road at that point and, also, the rutted condition of the road, which meant that ten kilometres had taken thirty minutes to drive.

Finally, we saw the headlights from the tow truck appear in the rear-view mirror.

We knew the tow truck driver would be mad, given the condition of the road, given that it was Sunday at dinnertime, but he was even more annoyed than we'd expected.

"CAA isn't going to pay for this," the lean bearded man muttered as he opened his door and strode toward our mired car.

"Oh," Mike said. "CAA didn't tell us that."

"CAA only covers maintained roads," he said with great feeling. "This isn't a road, it's an ATV trail. The road ended at the Reynolds Ponds."

"Well, I appreciate you coming to get us," I said.

"I almost turned around at that big washout back there," he said.

"I'm grateful you didn't," I said, realizing that I didn't know which of the big washouts he was talking about – there had been at least three. I'd made some bad decisions that day.

It took two backward tugs to get us out of the worst of the ruts. I was sitting in the car, running and in neutral, as the vehicle slowly surged out of the ruts. I got Mike to turn the car around, once we were definitely out of the ruts. I had to push the car when Mike got slightly stuck and felt how it moved with the pressure I applied. This was messy but satisfying, given that nothing we'd done all afternoon had made the car move an inch. We piled the sodden car mats in the back and, without another glance at the trees, the mud and the blowing poplar fuzz, slowly drove away as a caravan.

The tow truck had arrived at 6:30 p.m. but we didn't get back to the #1 Highway until just before eight o'clock.

As I drove around and into the ruts on the way back, I realized how out of it I'd been on the drive in. Instead of relying on my mapping app, which had been looking for the most direct route back to the highway instead of actual roads, I should have turned around and headed back the way I'd come. But I'd thought there would be a more direct route from the Ponds to the highway and I'd assumed that that's where the app was sending me. I had turned off that part of my brain and had concentrated on driving. In the past, the mapping app had asked me to turn right and then make a U-turn so I could drive left at a newish intersection instead of just turning left. When I wasn't tired or hungry, I would disregard what was clearly bad advice, even trash-talking Irish Siri a little – "What? No!" – as Irish Siri insisted that I turn right, that I return to the route. But that day, I needed help and I had trusted the app to provide it.

My bad decisions cost me $198, plus a $30 tip. That's ten hours at my desk, doing meaningful work at my non-profit rate. And that's just the cost of the tow truck, not the eleven hours I spent by the side of the road. Not Mike's time, either.

I kidnapped at least ten mosquitoes, which took turns landing on my hands/arms/face and tangling themselves in my hair as I drove.

ONCE I'D PAID the tow truck driver, who accepted my money and also another apology, I made Mike drive in front of me and I just followed him home. I was too tired for navigating.

The evening was pleasantly sunny, with a bright blue sky. I spotted an Adopt-a-Highway sign that said that this stretch of highway had been claimed by the Bearded Villains. I don't think the tow truck driver was a villain, but it made me smile.

And then, for the last twenty minutes, a blood-filled mosquito hovered where the windshield met the car. The evening sun made the blood in its abdomen – my blood – glow amber.

Red River Mudlarker

I AM DRIVEN to the riverbank by habit and history and temperament.

But in spring 2021, it was a post on Instagram by Manitoba Liberal Party leader Dougald Lamont – this being Winnipeg, he was my friend Laura Lamont's brother – that took me to a particular spot on the silty Red River that was almost completely covered with broken glass and pottery.

But this wasn't multinational Miller Genuine Draft or local Labatt beer bottles or even IKEA dishware, made in Romania.

It was fragments of hundred-year-old bottles with embossing, gone aqua or lavender in the sun. It was chips of china with flowers or abstracted patterns, flaring blue underwater or glinting gold from the mud.

Lamont's post was a lead-in to the Manitoba Liberals' *Plan for Green Growth and Renewal*, but sadly, I was most interested in what it revealed about the exposed riverbank:

I went for a walk down by the Red River behind confusion corner – across the river from Lyndale Drive. The water is very low and all the green you can [see] in the mud is broken glass bottles. They have been there a long time – some with Blackwoods stamped on the side, or a ceramic beer jug. A few years ago I sat down with an elder, Frank Tacan, who talked about how we take and take from the earth but we don't give back. For a greener future we need less waste. We need to tread more lightly on the earth. We need to stop treating rivers and lakes as sewage lagoons, and stop filling landfills. We need to recycle, compost and reuse but we need more than that. Giving back means preserving current wilderness, and letting wilderness and wildlife regenerate. Planting trees and forests, expanding wetlands, and promoting regenerative agriculture. We have a plan that does that, working together for renewal.

But "interested" is the wrong word: I felt almost "compelled."

The next day, I parked my dirty little Prius near the Winnipeg Rowing Club, where I'd spent a good chunk of my teens and twenties and walked across the bridge to the riverbank.

I was wearing the wrong shoes. I hadn't yet set up my mudlarking kit: the messenger bag, the gloves and gardening tools. And it was cooler than I thought it would be, which meant I was underdressed for a windy riverbank.

But it was glorious. The banks, the waterline, the bottom of the river: covered in shards of glass and sherds of pottery.

Was this treasure or only settler garbage?

I didn't know, but I felt broken open. I felt wild.

WHEN I WAS fifteen and sixteen and in a rowing shell, too many times, peering over my shoulder to see how close I was to the riverbank, I'd spot a man with his pants around his ankles between the trees, masturbating. It was the first time, besides my father, that I had seen a man naked.

When I was fifteen and sixteen and standing on the rowing club dock, wet with sweat and second-hand river water, in socked feet and glasses, I was pushed into the river as a joke, part of the usual roughhousing among teenagers. I remember trying to retrieve my glasses, the second or third time it happened, sinking down to the bottom and feeling around with my feet. Sobbing when I dragged myself out of the river, afraid to go home. My mother's rage, the mortgage, the meals to be cooked.

THERE ARE TWO kinds of people who inhabit the riverbanks, at least in Winnipeg.

Homeless people. Or, if you're someone versed in the language of harm reduction, the "unhoused" or even "people experiencing unsheltered homelessness." The Main Street Project defines "unsheltered" as anyone "without a home and not using an emergency shelter, instead staying in places like parks, bus shelters, entryways or vacant lots."

In pandemic Winnipeg, people had been setting up encampments on the banks of the river, in the thin beards of riverbank forests. Some camps had been occupied for years while others were occupied for a few weeks or a few months.

Abandoned homeless camps are thunderstorms of abandoned goods. Clothes, plastic bottles, takeout containers, bike parts. Sleeping bags, tents, plastic crates. Firepits and recycling bins, hauled to the riverbank and burned. The blackened trunks of trees, still standing. I have no interest in picking up this garbage, given the burnt knives and random syringes.

Fellow writer Sally Ito and I make dozens of trips to the riverbank with no problem, sharing the no man's land, but sometimes it doesn't work. Once, after veering away from one homeless man who emerged from a tent tucked under the bridge, unbuttoning his pants; after veering away from a man at the treeline who was taking off his shirt; after finally making our way down to the water, I realize that if we are confronted, there is nowhere to go. We would have to swim to the other bank.

"Mudlarkers." It's also a slippery word, borrowed from London's River Thames. Originally, mudlarking was a subsistence activity rooted in the nineteenth century; now, it's a hobby where people have to get a permit to look for items released by the Thames's anaerobic mud by the tides. Mudlarkers in the UK have found items dating as far back as the Roman, Saxon and Medieval periods, but the majority are from the Victorian and Edwardian eras.

The reason Sally and I haunt this particular stretch of the Red River is that there was a brewery here, or rather a series of breweries, with an associated glass recycling depot. The whole stretch is bordered by railroad tracks, which must have been very convenient for flinging chipped dishes, given the number of their patterns in the water. And there also seems to be construction waste, given the trees growing in and out of heaps of bricks and rusty metal scrap.

The oldest stuff we've found is from the 1880s, but the majority is from the 1910s and '20s. On the top part of the riverbank, closest to the bike path, there is household garbage from the 1930s and '40s.

training my eye
for man-made s
hapes in the mud,
ovals & cylinders,
lips & necks, for g
leam. I'm broken
but remember: gl
ass is sand, years
of 35-degree day
s focused on it, lik
e climate change o
nus. I know all broken bottles
look the same. I flip all face-down
white ceramics, mistaking the under
water nacre of dead bivalves for chunks
of hotelware: *goddamn it.* I miss the *slap*
& hiss of riverside beavers & geese until I
am almost upon them, flatten raccoon hand
prints with heavy boots as I fill my pockets w
ith surviving teacup handles, cut glass from s
ome granny's candy dishes. I forget that chin
a from China or Occupied Japan or even Chi
noiserie from England is clay & paint, peace
– AND wartime. I'm a settler garbage man, a
blasted inheritor, so far unable to pass up rus
ty clocks & bonfire glass. I pad my finds with
shed feathers & volunteer tomatoes, but win
d up with half my weight in clay-veined mud:
Red River gumbo. The ground is half cotton
wood leaves, half Slurpee straws. Like the sw
amp water of my teenage years – Coke & cre
am soda thinned out with Sprite – it's a stran
ge pleasure: *Sluuuurp.*

AT TWILIGHT, THE Red River's silty waters look darker.

I have been sloshing around for twenty minutes, halfway up my boots in the river. I feel good: engaged, exercized, excited about what I might find before full-dark.

And I look up to see someone on the path, looking down at me. I can't make out any details, except that it's a person.

"Are you all right?" the person asks. The voice is loud and strong. It sounds like the person is a woman.

"Yes, I'm fine," I call back. I am startled, but I'd never not-respond. This is what being human is: call and response.

I'm not sure what's she's worried about: Does it look like I'm committing suicide by wading into the river? Or that I'm trying to get away from someone on the riverbank?

"Be careful, okay?" she says.

"I will," I say.

And then she's gone, faded back into the twilight, walking toward the bridge or farther along the path. Or I disappeared her, looked back down into the building night in the river, at the shards of glass and sherds of pottery.

But I'm serious: I *am* careful. I'm a good swimmer, so even if I lost my footing and fell, I'd be able to swim to safety. I know this stretch of river: I know where the buildings are, where the bridge is. And I am only standing in half a foot of water.

I don't think Sally heard her, being twenty or thirty feet ahead of me. I don't mention it to her when we call it a night and walk together up the bank, giving the homeless encampment under the bridge a wide berth before crossing the bridge to our cars.

But I keep returning to that gesture. To that woman's clear voice on the riverbank.

WHEN I WAS twenty-one, having quit rowing for the student press, I went for a rambly walk opposite the rowing club, the side that was ambient train noise instead of lawn mowers. I was shocked to find all kinds of china and old glass glinting on the dirt path between the train tracks and the river. I filled my pockets, pleased to have found a place where all the rules of city living sagged, like the rope that secures a boat to a dock.

When I was thirty, Mike and I travelled to Yunnan province in China toward the end of the SARS epidemic. One hot day, walking from our hostel toward the lake we could see in the distance, we found ourselves on a dirt road next to farmers' fields. The road glinted with china, most of it with patterns. The day before we were due to leave, our guesthouse closed by government order and Mike got food poisoning. He had a high fever, which was the only symptom they were testing for in airports. Besides our first up-close experience with a pandemic, we brought home broken china from China.

I HESITATE TO use the word "mudlarker."

There's already enough of a disconnect to use the same word for two vastly different groups of people, separated by time and an economic gulf that stretches like the opposite banks of a river.

People trying to survive in nineteenth-century England, scavenging whatever goods fell or were dropped from the merchant vessels using the Thames to access London's markets.

The pandemic surge of people who can afford to spend time on the Thames foreshore with a trowel, consulting the tide map like a train schedule, oohing over a bone button or a glass bead.

It's illegal to sell anything mudlarked from the Thames, making contemporary mudlarking a bad subsistence activity. I would much rather refer to myself as a "bottle picker" than a "mudlarker," though since restarting my riverbank activities, I have gotten my hands on very few intact bottles.

training my fingers on glazed ceramics, the
porous orange of terracotta. Embossing &
gilt versus crazing & chips. Stained gla
ss scraps from lead-framed windo
ws blazing in new churches, ri
ch-man foyers. Ask myself:
Is a glass vase, ground
down, the same as a w
hite sand beach? Coul
d a clay pot be consid
ered a loan against a c
lay-loam riverbank? I d
ip my fingers in sewage &
industrial waste, dilute goose shit
& decaying plastics. I spend five months
standing in the river or tiptoeing its crumbling bank,
slicing fingertips on new edges of old glass. A dinner ser
vice for six hundred thousand smashed at my feet. Decemb
er, no snow: I prise embossed bottles out of frozen mud & hold
them aloft, the embossing a bottle digger's Braille. My red-headed
grandfather, newly returned from the Great War, his gonorrhea/gun
shot wound in the butt treated, could have sipped this beer, admiring the
wonky necks, the thick/thin glass, trapped bubbles. The glassmaker's moul
d showing. Could have smooched these machined lips. After retrieval, attem
pt to brush away the blackest asterisks of byssal threads of zebra mussels – f
irst with fingertips, then with nails. Nothing. At home, scrub at a hundred y
ears of grime, rust & burning. Try a bleach soak. Try white vinegar & ba
king soda, fizzling in the bin. Then, denture cleaner. I don't rememb
er if my grandfather had his own teeth. I can't ask my father – h
e's dead too. Return to the riverbank. Again. Pull on rubber b
oots impregnated with mud. Strap on my finds bag, gone
grey. Do my best to ignore the plastic, the bottles/
bags/wrapers/straws/bottlecaps everywhere,
all my generation: *Sigh* . . .

THE REASON THAT so much of the riverbank was exposed, back in May, is because floodplained Winnipeg is on our fourth or fifth drought year.

Each of those summers, we had weeks of wildfire smoke, the air grey, the sun orange even at midday. Winnipeg is a river city and, this summer, the water levels were so low that you could walk across the Assiniboine River without getting the tops of your boots wet.

Please understand: these were historic, climate-changed lows.

Despite the low river levels, the banks still act as corridors in and out of the city, as habitat, for all kinds of flora and fauna. This year, I shared space with families of beavers and geese, with eagles and raccoons, with old trees slowly toppling into the water and volunteer tomato plants, fruit almost glowing in the sun.

I spent as much time as I could on the riverbank. But try as I might, I couldn't wear through my riverbank compulsion.

I AM FORTY-EIGHT and walking to our usual spot on the riverbank, alone, and come upon a new homeless encampment. I don't want to walk into what is essentially someone's living room but I'm unsure of its boundaries. Seeing a young man standing on the top of a hill built of buried garbage and gumbo, staring warily, angrily, at me, I retreat back the way I'd come, tripping on underbrush, on what I recognize is fear.

I am forty-eight and the Winnipeg Police Service's River Patrol boat angles its way over to me and cuts the engine. "You all right?" they intone over the waves breaking over my feet. "Yes," I call. "Just looking for old bottles." They nod, faces carefully blank, and continue motoring along the river. The class judgment on me like a sunburn.

I SEE YOU TWO WOMEN STANDING ON THE RIVER-
BANK. WHAT THE FUCK ARE YOU DOING? GET THE
FUCK OUT OF THERE. (I don't know where the shouting is
coming from. I stop listening because I have to.)

(Embossed on all the bottles at my feet.) THIS BOTTLE IS OUR
PROPERTY ANY CHARGE MADE THEREFORE SIMPLY
COVERS ITS USE WHILE CONTAINING GOODS BOTTLED
BY US AND MUST BE RETURNED WHEN EMPTY

I AM FORTY-EIGHT and watching a school of rowing shells paddle
by. I am thinking of all my former selves, in and out of the water,
when suddenly: "Is that Ariel Gordon I spy?"

This being Winnipeg, it is a friend of mine, a political science
prof and serious brewer of beer who's been rowing as an adult longer than I ever rowed as a teenager and young adult. (He scavenges
neglected patches of backyard hops.)

"Hey, Peter Ives," I call out, squinting in the light that's gilding
the water between us, tucking the hair that has escaped my pony-
tail behind one ear. Feeling grubby but also occupied.

"Finding anything good?" he asks.

"So many things," I answer.

Not even sure if that's true.

Eating My Words

IN JULY 2022, I traded a copy of my book *Treed* to Shel Zolkewich, writer/bon vivant, for an armful of oyster mushrooms (*Pleurotus* sp.) growing from a broken tree on her property in Meleb, Manitoba, and some farm-fresh eggs.

I was thrilled that I'd somehow managed to turn my book about trees and mushrooms *into* mushrooms that I could eat (with a side of eggs . . .), instead of stupid money.

In the days after the trade, it became important to me that not a scrap of the food for which I'd bartered my book would go to waste. Eggs are not hard to consume – I have a hard-boiled or fried egg every morning and my daughter uses them in her baking. But oyster mushrooms spoil quickly, so I worked hard to eat every morsel of those oyster mushrooms, cleaned and sliced and cooked in oil.

I really liked the idea that I'd traded a container full of ideas, that I'd had the time to write down and rearrange those ideas for a bag full of mushrooms but also the time to find and pick those mushrooms.

The mushrooms themselves may not have lasted long, but the pleasure that I had traded my book for mushrooms lingered for weeks, long after I'd eaten, digested and excreted them.

I'd been working with Tom Nagy on a Zoom presentation for the Wolseley Community Gardens and his grow kits had already flushed the winter of 2021 with oyster mushrooms and lion's mane mushrooms that I'd somehow managed to grow myself. (As the youth say: 10/10, would recommend!)

And so, in the weeks after my trade with Shel, I asked Tom if he could help me feed my book to his mushrooms, by which I meant encourage them to grow onto/between its pages. My goal? To *eat* the mushrooms that had *eaten* my book.

I wanted to eat my own words.

WHEN I'M WALKING in the woods, when I'm surrounded by trees and mushrooms, lichen and moss, ferns and wildflowers, I feel connected to the world.

Like someone who's drunk or high, I'm terrible company.

I mostly just point out mushrooms growing on or under trees – even going so far as to go squat next to them, touching them gently – while murmuring about how happy I am. Over and over.

Like a child, I have terrible instincts when it comes to mushrooms. I'll wade into muddy ditches or into the bush, without thinking of my shoes/clothes. I'll sit directly on poison ivy if there's a mushroom I want to look at or photograph. I'll get covered in mosquito bites or turn myself into a climbing wall for wood ticks, despite a fulsome knowledge of West Nile or Lyme diseases.

I am particularly good at getting burrs in my hair.

I actually like getting filthy – it feels like I've had a proper adventure. Also, what's the point of clean clothes if not to get them dirty?

So the idea of "dirtying" a copy of *Treed* – a book about trees made of trees – made me happy.

July 13, 2022

Tom: Do you have a timeline for when you would like to have this completed and fruiting mushrooms?

Ariel: No timeline, per se. How long do you think it would take?

Tom: Not sure! Never tried to grow mushrooms out of a book before, haha. I would probably say ten to fourteen days from inoculate to fruit production? I can't see it taking longer than that, to be honest. It's not like we're trying to grow it out of a university textbook.

Ariel: [shares photo of an old copy of *Alice's Adventures in Wonderland* with mushrooms growing out of it] This was my original inspiration. People send it to me over and over, thinking I haven't seen it.

Tom: Haha. Oh yes. I have seen that one too. And those are psilocybin mushrooms growing out of that book. Very appropriate.

Ariel: Oh! I hadn't picked up on that.

IN OCTOBER 2020, I was chatting with Noelle Allen, my publisher, about how *Fungal* might have to change because of the pandemic.

When I'd come up with my plan in July of that year, it had involved a lot of travel, because I'd tried to set an essay in almost every Canadian province. I'd thought the pandemic would be over fairly soon, but that was really only the beginning, as the world changed, becoming smaller and larger all at once.

We'd discussed a few new essays, but I was really building up to a subject I was nervous about: psychedelic mushrooms. Otherwise known as shrooms or magic mushrooms, they all mean the same thing: any of the two hundred different mushrooms that contain psilocybin.

Health Canada's page for magic mushrooms on the "Controlled and illegal drugs" section of their website is slightly more precise, noting that the active ingredients in magic mushrooms are chemicals called psilocybin and psilocin, which is what psilocybin is converted to once it enters the body. It explains that these two drugs produce effects similar to LSD (a drug "made from lysergic acid, which is found in a fungus that grows on rye and other grains"): "Individuals using magic mushrooms experience hallucinations and an altered state of consciousness. Effects appear within 15 to 45 minutes and usually last for four to six hours."

Australia's Alcohol and Drug Foundation's definition of magic mushrooms is a little more expansive: "They are psychedelic drugs, which means they can affect all the senses, altering a person's thinking, sense of time and emotions. Psychedelics can cause a person to hallucinate, seeing or hearing things that do not exist or are distorted."

I was carting this information into my conversation with Noelle as though it was a hatful of mushrooms I'd collected and posted to a Facebook mushroom ID group: "Is anything here edible? Or a magic mushroom?"

"So . . . the other essay is about *not* wanting to take magic mushrooms. About not being religious or even spiritual but being an ecstatic, which I hadn't realized until someone remarked on it," I wrote. "By which I mean, I am made so happy by being immersed in even the smallest patch of woods and finding mushrooms."

Basically, I really didn't want to take psychedelics and write about it, like I'd seen in two recent books. I am someone who is lucky enough to not be on any medication – I don't even take vitamins. Neither do I take very many recreational drugs, partly because I watched my father get drunk at dinnertimes in the years before my parents' separation, which made me a bit leery of addiction. And it's already hard enough living with my chosen vices: caffeine, sugar, salt, fat and carbs. I already talk about tea like it's my beloved – my partner wooed me with cups of takeout tea, doctored with lots of cream and sugar.

From a purely practical standpoint, recreational drugs – legal and illegal – are also expensive, complicated and time-consuming, in terms of getting them, consuming them and recovering from them.

All of which is to say: I like the strategies and ways of being-in-the-world that I've evolved so far.

Noelle's response, when it came, was reassuring. "It never occurred to me that you'd try that, to be honest."

It was classic Noelle: words infused with common sense and, also, a wryness that I appreciated. Noelle was used to talking to writers in the middle of manuscripts like they were nervous horses. *Neigh.*

TO MY MOTHER's chagrin, I am also *not* interested in organized religion, even though I grew up in the Anglican and then the United Church.

But on Xmas Eve I go to my mother's church to listen to the carols I sang as a child. She sings in the choir, and the choir performs from the choir loft, so I get the experience of hearing but not seeing her. (Which, come to think about it, is sort of how people describe their relationship with various gods . . .)

The other thing I like about those services is the candlelight. As people enter the church, the ushers pass out tall thin white candles with cardboard guards to protect hands/pews/carpeting from dripping wax. The candles aren't used until the very end of the service, when the ushers dim the lights. The minister lights a few candles and then people turn to their neighbours, passing the flame between candles.

In a few minutes, the whole church is dark and light. It feels like community.

And then everyone sings "Silent Night" in their imperfect voices.

It is everything I need from Xmas. Nostalgia, familiarity and connection: my voice blending with other people's voices.

But I have no interest in attending church outside of Xmas Eve. And those carols? The lyrics and melodies are familiar but oh-so-strange, reread and reconsidered as an adult. I can't imagine being that praiseworthy of anything besides a mushroom. Or a leaf. Or the pattern that fallen crabapples make on a cobblestone path.

I am also not interested in anything anyone would describe as spiritual. I don't pray or meditate, though forest bathing is what I imagine those practices feel like to believers/practitioners.

I don't not-believe in a higher power. It just doesn't even occur to me to ask questions about whether or not there *is* a higher power. And while I respect people who find meaning and comfort in either organized religion or other spiritual practices, I actively avoid conversations with them about their faith or faith journeys. (When my daughter wanted to go to a Mennonite Church of Can-ada sleepaway camp that had bible study every day because her best friend had signed up, I agreed but told her: "No God-talk when you get back, child . . .")

But if I had to sum it up, I'd say that the woods – which is to say, any patch of land with more than three trees on it – are my church.

I know that when I finish a walk, my mood will have shifted, like weather. I know I'll feel pleasantly worn out in my body but my mind will, for a short time, work better. I know I only understand parts of the complex systems that bind us all together, but I feel those connections every single time I spend time outside.

SPEAKING OF NOSTALGIA, I grew up on scratch-and-sniff stickers, which I compiled into albums and traded with my friends. We didn't just sniff, we huffed, fascinated by fake-o chemical versions of real food.

At forty-nine, I am *deeeeeep* into middle-age, so didn't hop on my daughter's generation's trend of buying/affixing durable but sadly non-smelly stickers to laptops, reusable water bottles and phones.

But then my favourite nature artist on Instagram, Jenny Liski, who goes by Scout Paper Goods and is based in Edmonton, released some of her gorgeous moss/lichen/mushroom illustrations as stickers. So for almost a year I had her Madame's Pixie Cup on the back of my phone case. I still have her Elegant Sunburst Lichen and Nodding Thread Moss on my laptop. Next to the Elegant Sunburst Lichen is an ugly/beautiful sticker, which has the ultimate combination, the final boss, of my two love/hates. It's square and brown and is designed to resemble a U.S. Parks sign. It has a small V of geese, a single large goose and three mushrooms crowded together under the parks logo. It reads: DO NOT FEED HALLUCINOGENS TO THE GEESE.

So I wouldn't be taking magic mushrooms in service of my book, but the thought of Canada geese, already prone to shouting and bad decisions like roosting in garden boxes or on asphalt rooftops, off their tits on shrooms, made me chortle.

IN FALL 2020, Noelle could have left our conversation about magic mushrooms at that, but she elaborated, which was like a soft hand placed softly on my soft horse nose: "Just let the psychedelic mushrooms go, I think we've lots of other ground to cover. And we can be personal without getting experimental that way."

Of course, I then had to argue against my own position: "I feel like it's something people will ask about."

"Probably, but so be it. I think there have been lots of writers investigating mind-altering substances and writing about it in the past," Noelle continued. "I figure it's been done. We don't have to go over it again. And is it really that interesting?"

I thought about Timothy Leary, the American '60s counterculture icon and psychologist, who took psychedelics alongside his research subjects.

"Turn on, tune in, drop out" indeed.

WHEN I ASK around, I discover that several friends and family members are microdosing psychedelic mushrooms, which means that they are taking very small amounts of psilocybin regularly.

A writer friend in Saskatchewan confides that he been taking psilocybin for three months: "I don't want to get high; I just want to function."

He tells me that he started microdosing after reading Michael Pollan's book *How to Change Your Mind: What the New Science of Psychedelics Teaches Us About Consciousness, Dying, Addiction, Depression, and Transcendence.*

"I've been on antidepressants for thirty years and worry about their side effects and the fact that they barely keep me functioning. Pollan makes a good case for their therapeutic use, in both microdoses and larger doses as well. I thought it couldn't hurt to try them. I did take a couple of large doses, but without a therapist to guide me through the experience, that was a little frustrating and rather ineffective. The microdosing has been key to a complete shift or uplift in mood and general functioning."

My friend says buying his psilocybin capsules from Canadian online dispensaries is easy: the only difference is that he has to pay by e-transfer, because apparently you can't use PayPal or a credit card to buy illegal substances.

He says he can't believe how much better he feels, after only three months: "Even when I have a bad day, I don't experience the black dog of depression looming on the horizon. I'm better able to deal with frustrations, I think, although I'm not perfect at it. My mood is much better. I've never felt this good. I tell anyone who confesses to being depressed to try them."

But microdoses of psilocybin aren't miracle cures; like every other therapeutic treatment, there can be side effects.

"The first time I took them, I got confused about the dose and took two capsules, which made me feel jumpy and jangly. I had a nap and that passed. And sometimes I feel kind of jazzed, as if I've had too much coffee. In fact, on the days when I take the dose (I take it twice a week), I restrict myself to one coffee, because I don't like that speedy feeling at all."

When my friend recently started seeing a therapist, they had an initial telephone conversation. He told her that he'd been microdosing, to which she responded: "The cure for depression is movement and psychedelics." She told him that she's just completed training on using psychedelics in her practice, which means that her clients will be able to get psilocybin from their family doctor on prescription and she will guide them through their experience. He'd like to take that journey with her, hopefully this summer.

"Her openness to my microdosing is really the reason I wanted to see her," he said. "I was expecting to be shut down and her response was a pleasant surprise."

I am so glad that my friend and the other people I know have found tools that are helping them, given a medical system that sometimes feels like it is stumbling along, post-pandemic.

A recent CBC story about the Naut sa mawt Centre for Psychedelic Research at Vancouver Island University in BC said that researchers there are looking at the ways that psychelics could help treat intergenerational trauma in Indigenous peoples. This research is in addition to their current work, using psilocybin to treat distress in people that are dying, depressed or who have Alzheimer's. They also use MDMA to treat fibromyalgia and ketamine to treat firefighters with PTSD.

And I'm glad for all of it. Anything that helps people survive their lives, to feel connected to the world and to each other, is valuable.

It just isn't for me. It's a medicine I don't need, at least at this point in my life.

July 26, 2022

Inoculating *Treed* with mushroom spawn was like making a lasagna or a layer cake.

When I arrived at Tom's apartment, the book was splayed, face down, in a tub of water, secured by three Mason jars also filled with water.

According to the Bookmark Alignment Chart, which rates the various ways people mark their places in books, leaving a book face down is Neutral Evil. I'm frequently Neutral Evil and even sometimes the worst of the worst, Chaotic Evil, which is dog-earing pages.

The book had been in Neutral Evil for a full day, in preparation for inoculation.

Next to the tub was a heaping bowl of wheat kernels that had been inoculated with oyster mushroom spawn. If you didn't look closely, you'd think that it was high-fibre cereal or hardcore granola or even a deconstructed puffed wheat square.

Tom knows this is oyster mushroom spawn but doesn't remember exactly what kind it is. He produces several varieties of oyster mushroom grow kits from strains he purchases, including black pearl king oysters and pink oysters, which are a beautiful peachy pink. He also developed a strain of his own in 2019, which he calls the Wolseley Oyster.

"These beauties were cloned from a wild oyster growing from an elm stump in the Wolseley neighbourhood of Winnipeg," Tom wrote in an Instagram post introducing the strain. "A tissue sample was taken from the wild mushrooms and cultured on agar for several generations before being transferred to liquid culture and grain spawn for long term storage."

I was hoping that what we'd infested my book with was the Wolseley Oyster, just because that dovetailed with the things I'd written about. Trees and mushrooms, as opposed to this book's focus, mushrooms and trees. So different!

While we worked, Tom commented he had been nervous about so mistreating a book, but I told him books are just containers for ideas. I tried to explain how exciting the idea of reusing that container – like a margarine tub – was for me.

Manitoba is home to six large historical populations: the Cree, Anishinaabe and Métis people, and settler populations of Jewish, Ukrainian and Mennonite people. This is, of course, in addition to the dominant French and English cultures that colonized Canada. So I grew up buying and eating frozen perogies, using Yiddish-isms like "shmutz" or "klutz" in everyday speech, and wearing Métis "ceinture fléchées" during Festival du Voyageur, our Franco-Manitoban winter festival. So understand that I mean no disrespect when I tell you that the local way to refer to repurposed margarine tubs is "Ukrainian Tupperware." It speaks to the desire to use anything useful until it is worn out. I imagine the thought process of babas are as follows: "Why buy fancy plastic containers for food storage, for sending home leftovers with my grown children after Sunday dinner that I might never get back, when I can use a margarine tub?" I try to embody that lifestyle myself: use and reuse, gift and regift and don't buy new unless I really need to. Like a margarine container that wasn't designed for long-term storage of anything besides, say, margarine, my book wasn't designed to grow mushrooms, but it will probably work.

We squeezed out the excess water and set the book on Tom's workbench. And then, using a soup spoon, we spread a thick layer of myceliated grain every twenty pages or so. (The Bookmark Alignment Chart says that putting a leaf in a book to mark your place is Chaotic Neutral. Another version of the chart I found says that Chaotic Neutral is "leaves book open, face down, at last page read" and Chaotic Evil is "rips out each page once it's been read." In the world of the bookmark alignment meme, growing mushrooms on a book, where mushrooms *eat* the book, would probably be considered *Evil Evil*.)

Once we were done, we used three elastic bands to secure the bookshroom together, at least until the fungi had infiltrated and bound together the pages with mycelia. We put the final product in a big Ziploc bag and set it on the shelf with Tom's other mushroom kits, waiting for the mushroom culture to completely colonize the book before transferring it into his fruiting chamber, which is an enclosed space with consistent airflow/moisture.

While Tom thinks we'll be able to grow mushrooms on my book, he's not exactly sure how things will progress: we might not get three flushes of mushrooms, for instance.

My main take-away from this session is that feeding a block of paper to mushrooms – as opposed to shredded cardboard or newspaper or woodchips or sawdust – is equivalent to a diet consisting entirely of potato chips.

MY WRITER FRIEND from Saskatchewan puts me in touch with his therapist, who is a social worker with a Bachelor of Social Work from UBC and a Master's from the University of Regina.

Celeste Seiferling describes herself as "a clinical counsellor, sexual health educator, mental health advocate, dancer and aerialist, intersectional feminist." She has training in Trauma Informed Practice, Somatic Experiencing, Anti-Oppressive Practice, Harm Reduction Education, 2SLGBTQ+ counselling and Dance/Movement Therapy. Seiferling agreed to talk to me about psychedelics, specifically how she had sought out training on how to use them in her therapeutic practice.

> I have personally experienced and witnessed the profound effects of psychedelics in my own life and was very curious about what this would look like in a therapeutic context. Before I started my training, I already had clients who were using psychedelics in various ways, and I was helping them to integrate their learning and healing, so I also wanted more information and clarification on how to do this in the best way possible. I very much believe in a holistic model of healing, and so whatever we can add to our tool kits to help folks feels really exciting to me.

By tool kit, Seiferling means techniques like talk therapy and cognitive-behavioural therapy (or CBT), eye movement desensitization and reprocessing (or EMDR) and drugs like SSRIs. She's excited to fully incorporate psychedelics into her practice.

It means that we can give people more hope. That there is another option when therapy feels like it isn't enough. When people feel like they have hit a plateau with their therapist, or when they are struggling to find a good therapist. Or when their psychiatrist has deemed them 'treatment resistant,' which is a really disheartening and hopeless label.

It means that we might be able to get people into more sustainable states of safety and connection, which is often what is missing with different kinds of support. It means we might be able to support people to get off their long-term pharmaceuticals, and give them a new sense of empowerment over their brains and bodies. And that sounds really exciting.

Seiferling says many people, like my friend, have started their journey with psychedelics by microdosing: "Micro-dosing has been a good place for some people to start with these drugs, and even there I have seen really big, positive shifts. It helps to gently move the depression away, to create more space for balance, improved mood, better focus and creativity."

But taking a larger dose of psychedelics is where Seiferling has seen the most change in her patients.

A therapeutic dose (2.5 to 7 grams) has many benefits – when people are properly prepared and supported. The most recent studies have been done on end-of-life anxiety with cancer patients and depression, but there are benefits for many mental health struggles, from PTSD to addiction to eating disorders. These drugs were heavily researched in the 1960s, showing promise for healing from many of the mental illnesses people were struggling with – but the U.S. government shut it down in 1965 – thus beginning the war on drugs. Studies were restarted in the early 2000s, at Johns Hopkins, researching psilocybin's effect on end-of-life anxiety, quitting smoking, alcohol abuse and depression.

There are a lot of places in therapy where people get stuck, where it is not possible to get out of our own way – even with the most successful evidence-based practices with the best therapists. Our brains and bodies work really hard to develop protective patterns that actually cause us harm when we are no longer in need of their protection. Psychedelics do a good job of cutting through our own shit to help us see what is really going on, and how we can choose to do things differently. They give us new eyes to see and understand, and they also give us the capacity in our bodies to reprocess some of the hardest stuff we have ever gone through.

We also get the gift of neuroplasticity for about a month after a large dose – which basically means that our brains are more malleable and can form new connections and networks. This can help us to change our behaviour and our mindsets in really profound ways. This is where we get big changes like no longer relying on substances to cope with our negative feelings, having a new perspective on anxiety or OCD, and having a new sense of how we think about our body, and forming new habits and patterns around eating.

NOTHING IS NEW. The world and our thinking is circular, cyclical.

Just before *Treed* came out in May 2019, a dozen or more people sent me that picture of Lewis Carroll's *Alice's Adventures in Wonderland* with a gorgeous cluster of mushrooms growing out of it. The photographer's name had been pruned away – as usually happens on the Internet – but the caption that had somehow attached itself to the image was that an old water-damaged book had been found like this. (I found the photographer, a scientist in a red state, who confirmed that he grew the mushrooms on an old copy of the book and then photographed it for an art project. When it went viral, he was too frightened to assert its origins, given the possible professional repercussions for him.)

That was when I first decided I wanted to grow mushrooms on my book. At the time, I was following Jarrett Moffatt of Prairie Oysters on Instagram, whose slogan was "Do you Sell Mushrooms or Cow Testicles?"

I reached out to him, asking if he'd be up for adding my book to his basement grow-chamber. He was too busy, driving around boxes of fresh mushrooms to restaurants and other interested parties on his scooter, but he made me a counter-offer: "What if I gave you a little mushroom spawn and you did it yourself? All you do is put the book in a Ziploc bag, wet it, and watch it grow."

The only issue was that it was June and I was about to go on a book tour for *Treed* and so would be out of town for three weeks. Moffat said that it would take a month to get going anyway and that he couldn't guarantee it would work if I waited until I got back.

So I drowned my book, then put it in a Ziploc and propped it up next to our range, in a spot where it was unlikely to be knocked over by roaming/lonely cats.

When I got back, I checked in with Moffatt: "After nearly three weeks, there's some condensation in the Ziploc bag and I can see white mycelium growing on the bottom of the book. Do I need to do anything else at this point?"

"Not bad, not bad! Let's see what happens. It may have needed a bit more spawn but until there's green showing up you'll be in great shape."

"Okay, will do. Does it need to be in the sun?"

"Mycelium grows in the dark, haha."

Sadly, the conglomeration that was now my book only produced a few small mushrooms in September and then stalled. I had never grown mushrooms before and didn't really know what to do, so I let everything dry out and then put my bookshroom on a shelf.

"Oh well," I told myself. "I tried."

I'd mostly forgotten this experience by the summer of 2022, three long pandemic years later.

THE NEXT LULL in my conversation with Noelle was a pleasurable one. I felt I had been seen and understood, even in my neighing-and-pawing-the-ground state, even with all the changes to "The Plan."

Then Noelle typed again: "If you're ever in doubt about me expecting you to do ridiculous things to write about, don't hesitate to ask me."

Suddenly, I wasn't a jittery horse, but a truffle dog/pig, intent on a buried lump of tuberous fungi in Italy. Better, I was myself again.

Grinning, I typed, "ARIEL YOU MUST TAKE DRUGS FOR THIS BOOK TO BE A SUCCESS."

IN EARLY AUGUST 2022, Tom sent me video bookshroom updates.

August 1, 2022

Tom: So I moved the book from the Ziploc bag that it was in because it wasn't getting any fresh air exchange. I don't know why I didn't think of that before. And so I just sealed it in one of these bags. As you can see, it's pretty puffy, there's some positive pressure in there, but obviously it's breathing now, which is great. There are some fluffy patches of mycelium, obviously it's all fogged up. Oh yeah, you can see it there pretty good. So there's definitely action happening . . . we're well on our way.

August 4, 2022
Tom: So as you can see, the mycelium has started to reach the top of the book now. Yeah, it's pretty foggy in there. Looking really good on this side too. Nice and steamy and humid in there. Yah, we're going. Hard to say when it'll be done at this point or if it'll burst through the top of the cover or if it'll kind of go from the open sides all the way up and around. Yeah, it's going.

August 12, 2022
Ariel: I'm heading out of town today for two weeks. If I don't catch the first flush of bookshrooms, that's fine. Just take pictures.

Tom: Oh that's right! And thanks for reminding me . . . although probably not great timing because your book just starting fruiting! Likely a couple of days ago, actually. I didn't notice them right away but they are in the fruiting chamber now and so some should mature just fine. And yes! I'll save them for you (likely dried) and take lots of photos. They caught me off guard because I expected the whole cover of the book to be consumed . . . but it appears they just went for the insides and were content with that.

Ariel: It looks different than I expected!

Tom: The mushrooms are growing all weird because I should have taken them out of the bag earlier, haha . . . but they should figure themselves out.

CONFESSION #1: I took magic mushrooms once, when I was travelling in Indonesia in my twenties.

Mostly, I wanted to eat everything and have sex with everyone. The person I was doing mushrooms with admitted afterward that she had given us a huge dose by accident. She spent the entire "trip" steering me away from things I was quite obviously leering at: food and men. She also was convinced she'd peed her pants and so elaborated several subtle-to-her methods of checking to see if she'd in fact urinated.

It wasn't a bad experience, per se, but it wasn't anything I wanted/needed to do again.

I ASKED SEIFERLING whether or not it is important for people to have someone guiding them when they take large doses of psychedelics.

This part is incredibly important, and likely the missing piece for a lot of folks who are using psychedelics in their healing practices. Because the use of psychedelics is still in the grey area of legal, so it can be hard to find good, knowledgeable guides. Having a co-sitter helps to set the container that grounds the experience and establishes safety. It is really helpful if you have built a relationship with this person, so that you know and trust them, because if you don't, that will definitely affect your experience.

When trauma is interpersonal (which nearly all of it is), then the healing has to be interpersonal as well. As much as we may try, healing cannot happen in isolation. It is so important to have your nervous system believe that people can be safe, especially when you are in a vulnerable state – which you are when you have consumed a large dose of any psychedelic. If you don't feel safe, then you will fight the come-up of the drug, and that can be more painful and harmful than trusting and allowing it to do what it is meant to do.

Having someone with you helps prevent re-traumatization, by helping to co-regulate when things get difficult, to move you through fight-or-flight states. They can help to get you unstuck by changing your location, or using sensory stimulation to remind you where you are.

Even going to the bathroom alone is hard when you have consumed a large dose, so having someone there for your physical safety is important too!

August 15, 2022
Ariel: Any mushrooms on my book yet? I feel like a mushroom nag but oh well.

Tom: Haha . . . yes! They are maturing and might even be ready to pick tonight. The weather was really warm over the weekend so everything matured quite fast. [Tom sends pictures of clusters of white oyster mushrooms growing out of each corner of the book.]

Ariel: Those are amazing!!

Tom: They would look much nicer if they grew in cooler weather . . . they matured super fast over the weekend and I was out of town too, which didn't help. Will pick and get them dried this week.

CONFESSION #2: THE first time I inoculated my book with mushroom spawn, I did it because the concept pleased me but also because I have an Internet addiction and wanted to take pictures of it.

Three years later, with three successful mushroom kits behind me, the pandemic mostly sort-of over, I wanted to do it again because I had already digested *Treed* – launching it, touring it, talking about it – and liked the symbolism of having mushrooms digest my book too.

I wondered if I'd get enough for a good meal, body and soul.

I AM SITTING in my daughter's therapist's waiting room when my writer friend David Yerex Williamson, a professor at the University College of the North, posts a poem.

Today, I declined to give the closing prayer / for a meeting of poets / it's not that I don't believe in prayer / poetry is a kind of prayer / all my teenage hymns for hers / it is more that I don't believe / how prayer works / if it works at all / birthing a child is a kind of prayer / supplication through adoration / and all that comes with so much submission / creative non-fiction is a kind of prayer / cs, repentance, our version of the sins / we believe / walking is kind of prayer / pausing before a river, a kind of devotion / writing a letter, building a house / planting, casting nets / standing alone in an alley at night / because we have wars, poverty, disease / great men and better women / teenage hymns and hers / we need prayer / especially when it doesn't work.

I thanked David for his poem in the comments beneath his post. And then immediately messaged him privately, asking if I could transplant the poem into this essay, like a clipping I was gluing into my notebook, like a clump of ferns I wanted to move to my garden, hoping it would survive the transplant shock.

The poem reminded me that I hadn't looked up ecstatics yet, so I went looking for a definition. Specifically, I went to the 1985 compact edition of the *Oxford English Dictionary*, which my art critic friend Amy Karlinsky gave me when they were moving. The main definition of the adjectival form of "ecstatic" – found on page 831 of the first volume – is "Of the nature of trance, catalepsy, mystical absorption, stupor, or frenzy," followed by "Of persons: subject to experiences of this kind." And then: "One who is subject to fits of ecstasy." Of course, "ecstasy" used to be a word with spiritual connotations but now has come to mean "chiefly positive emotion." It's also the name of a hallucinogenic/stimulant street drug that also goes by the name MDMA, one I'd never tried.

I had two thoughts: First, that I resemble that remark.

Second, that this is my first time owning a version of the *Oxford English Dictionary*. Even the compact edition is huge, with tiny script I had to take a photo of and then zoom in to read.

It would probably grow a ginormous crop of mushrooms.

THE FIRST WEEK of October 2022, Tom messages me again.

October 1, 2022
Tom: Your book has finally decided to go for round two! With even more pins than before. and this time since it has been in the grow space this whole time they are actually all forming properly.

Ariel: Oh cool! Can I come visit this week sometime?

Tom: You bet! Would you like to come by when they will be ready to pick? I could also hand off the dried ones to you as well?

Ariel: Sounds good!

October 3, 2022
Ariel: How are those book pins doing?

Tom: Good! They are small, but they look nice. Would you like to come by tomorrow?

Ariel: Yes I could come tomorrow but I could also wait a day or two if you prefer (or if you think the mushrooms would get any bigger . . .)?

Tom: At this point, probably not. The edges are beginning to flare out, which signals that they are pretty much ready. Your book appears not to be particularly nutritious, haha.

NOTHING IS NEW. The world and its processes are circular, cyclical.

When I was at the 2019 hometown launch for *Treed*, at McNally Robinson in Winnipeg, and taking questions from the crowd after my reading was done, my friend James, the air traffic controller husband of my writer-friend Anita Daher, put up his hand.

He was grinning like a devil, so I knew I was in for it.

"So you say you love trees but your book is printed on paper, from trees, right?" James asked.

People who knew him, who knew me, groaned in pleasurable discomfort. "That Jimmy!" I could hear them thinking, but also, "That's actually a good question." And "I wonder what she is going to say?"

My answer is the same now as then: printed books are the most durable containers we've found for ideas, lasting hundreds or even thousands of years. Ebooks are great and have accessibility features that make them absolutely necessary, but you never need to plug in a paper book. You can slip a paper book in your bag for a day or a month and its riches are always and instantly available, unless you smoosh a banana into its pages. Books can also be undone by slippery fingers in the bath – the pages rippled like sand at the bottom of a lake – by floods and housefires, but they live longer as containers for ideas than we do.

What's lovely about them is that one copy isn't worth much as a work of art, as individuals. Books are to ideas as mushrooms are to fungi: a fruiting body. A mode of transmission or dispersal. There are hundreds or even thousands of copies of each book and each copy is easily replaceable. For instance, there are thirty-nine copies of *Treed* in libraries across North America, in places I will never have the chance to visit, but I like to think there are invisible lines radiating from those far-off shelves back to my buzzing brain and my little patch of woods.

I would be happier if we could find something besides wood pulp to make paper from, but I can't imagine what it would be. If I could choose, I'd like this book to be printed on hemp fibre. But I'd also like it to be printed on the grey-white-black walls of wasps' papery nests or the herbivore green of elephant dung.

I like that at least one copy of this book has been broken down by fungi the same way that a tree is broken down into sawdust and then soil in the forest.

October 4, 2022

Tom's bedroom/lab is sunny and breezy, the boulevard elm outside the window dappling the light but still letting lots in. This is probably the nicest time to be alive in Winnipeg, for a mushroom enthusiast at least. Golden light and mushrooms everywhere – the boulevard, anywhere there are trees, from a pocket park to a cemetery to a big regional park – especially if there has been some rain.

My book is sealed shut, colonized by clusters of delicate ivory mushrooms, more and less of itself. I gently remove the fourteen mushrooms – one large mushroom, five medium mushrooms and seven small mushrooms. I line them up on Tom's stainless-steel workbench and let the light play over them.

I leave with the mushrooms but leave the transformed book behind. We decide that we're going to try for a third flush, which is standard with mushroom grow kits.

I almost forgot about the bookshrooms, but that weekend, I pulled them out of the fridge.

I sautéed the fresh mushrooms in olive oil until the gills were browned, then put them on top of a toasted seedy bagel, while reading the Saturday books section in the *Winnipeg Free Press*.

If you're keeping track, I'm consuming book reviews printed on paper while *also* consuming a mushroom that consumed a book printed on paper about trees.

I have to admit that I still don't know whether I've closed the loop or not. I don't know what symbolic mushrooms are supposed to taste like, but these tasted liked good fresh oyster mushrooms, cooked in such a way that their flavour was at the forefront. If I hadn't known they'd been grown from a book, I wouldn't have guessed it from their appearance or taste.

TOWARD THE END of my interview with Seiferling, I asked if there was anything she'd like to tell me about using psychedelics as treatment for mental health issues.

"Just a thought for those who are still feeling fearful or hesitant; I'd invite you to ask yourself where that fear comes from. What is telling you that this is something to resist? What informs your awareness of what drugs are 'safe' and which are 'harmful'? Is it possible to interrogate those thoughts and beliefs? Is it possible to move a little bit further toward curiosity rather than judgment?"

I was shaken by this response. Maybe my not-wanting-to-take-mushrooms-and-write-about-it wasn't as straightforward as I'd thought. So I asked Seiferling: Did she think it would be worthwhile for someone like me to take psychedelics? What did she think I would (or could) get out of it?

My gut answer to your question is that I absolutely do not think everyone needs to take psychedelics, and also that most people could maybe learn something from them. Similar to most things in therapy – will it benefit most people to go outside more often, feel more connected to nature, and move their body? Yes. Does that mean I am going to tell everyone that they have to do those things? Absolutely not. Each individual person gets to decide what is best for them in their life.

And lots of people have good and valid reasons to not take any substances. Even those that could potentially be beneficial. Similar to how people have good and valid reasons to not take SSRIs or other anti-anxiety/depressants.

It would depend on what your intentions are as to how the medicine would benefit you. Could psychedelics enhance your experiences in nature, or connect you more to yourself? Maybe. Could it make you see yourself, or the world differently? Perhaps. Could it help you move through things you may not be aware that you are carrying? Probably. Does that mean you have to explore them? No.

If it feels like a medicine you don't need, then you can listen to that. Trust your own intuition above all else. Just check in to see if it is your intuition, and not your fear – as those two things get confused sometimes.

IN NOVEMBER 2022, I find the bag of dried bookshrooms in the cupboard and add them to a bowl of ramen alongside dried wood ear mushrooms and seaweed. I don't recall tasting them specifically, bathed in the fat/salt/umami of the soup. They'd just turned into food.

I don't know if I'd want to eat mushrooms from a bookshroom every day. I'm not sure if they would be safe to eat, absorbing some of the chemicals from the process that turns wood pulp into paper, from the inks. But I'm sure I've eaten worse things.

In the end, I didn't change my mind about taking psychedelic mushrooms. Maybe that makes me the ridiculous thing. But my response to the anxiety and ennui of the climate crisis, late-stage capitalism and the middle-end of the pandemic has been to try to build a life that feels as meaningful and as interesting as I can make it, without hurting other people. While I feel obligations to my family and my community, I only do things that I want to do. I try not to let guilt or fear make choices for me. When I work for money, I only do it for groups and organizations that I believe in, trading a lower salary for meaningful work.

It helps that I am by nature both easily amused and enthusiastic about the world. It helps that most of the activities I love are cheap/free. It helps that I am part of a lively and generous community of writers and artists, friends and colleagues, that I can rely on and where I can in turn offer my support, which is satisfying for me. My one regret is that I am not more of an activist for the things I believe in: a just society, a planet that is healthy and balanced. But I can honestly say that I'm doing my best as an artist and a woman and a member of a family. And that's all I can do.

I TOOK BACK custody of my mushroom-infested copy in February 2023, which included the third flush of mushrooms.

It had been a small flush, not really worth picking, so Tom had just let it dry out once it had finished growing. The bookshroom, a mix of paper and dried-out oyster mushroom mycelium, of intentions and ideas, had been sitting on his coffee table for months as a conversation piece.

The process took seven months, from dropping off a pristine copy in July to picking up the consumed one in February.

I thought it was a beautiful object: the dried mushrooms were the same yellowy beige as the cover, somehow. It looked petrified, transformed in a way that I hadn't expected. I was reluctant to dissect it at first – besides my royalty statements, it was the best artefact of a life in writing and publishing – but my curiosity got the better of me. When you drop a book in the bathtub, you can still read it, even though the paper of its pages have become wavy, even unmanageable. I wanted to know: Would any part of the bookshroom still function like a book?

So I went and got a hammer, some screwdrivers, a box cutter, scissors and two small jewellery-making pliers. It looked like I was going to try to break into a safe, not a bookshroom. It felt like I was bringing a knife to a gunfight, but I reminded myself: there are no best-practices for bookshroom dissection.

In the end, I mostly used the box cutter to break the seal between the mycelium and the pages and a flathead screwdriver to pry open a few of the places we'd put the infested grain.

But first I weighed it, on the baking scale my daughter got for her birthday.

In 1907, a doctor tried to prove his hypothesis that human souls had a measurable weight. He weighed people before and after death and found in one case that there was a difference of twenty-one grams between a living and dead human. Called the "21 Gram Experiment," it has since been widely disproved for a host of reasons, but the idea persists.

So an uninfested copy of the book weighed 353 grams, while the fungi-eaten version, that could kind-of sort-of be read, weighed 366 grams. The mycelia sealing my book shut weighed only thirteen grams!

That's three or four therapeutic doses of psychedelic mushrooms, if you're keeping track. Or almost three-quarters of a human soul.

Rotten

Result: High grade squamous intraepithelial lesion. What it means: Moderate to severe abnormal changes were seen. This result is more serious. What you should do: Make sure your health care provider has made a colposcopy appointment for you. – *What you need to know about preventing cervical cancer*, CervixCheck, CancerCare Manitoba

Q: How do I recognize if my tree is infected? A: Look into the tree canopy, wilting of leaves is usually the first stage of DED, followed by yellowing then browning of the leaves. If you are unsure please call 311 for a Forestry Technician to inspect. – *Frequently Asked Questions: Dutch Elm Disease*, Urban Forestry, City of Winnipeg

ON A SULTRY evening in July 2021, I heat-wave-sit on my front steps, hoping to catch a stray breeze. My legs are folded over my cervix, a rotten egg I cradle in my lightly used loins – thousands of gametes, one child – for fear of breaking it.

Dud eggs – eggs that just never hatched – are like bombs, their terrible smell, their blossoming rot just barely contained by their shells. I know my cervix isn't a dud or even a booby trap, but I still I clench like I have an achingly full bladder, like I'm about to Frankenstein up the stairs to the only bathroom, only to find that someone is already using it, is firmly installed.

Fifteen feet away, my 110-year-old boulevard elm is glorious, full of sap and leaves that reach over the house, with a dense spread of three stories. It has scars on its trunk from generations of snow- and earth-moving machines, leftover nails and industrial staples from years of tree-banding, abandoned now. Best practices.

In May and June some years, worms hang from its bare branches over the front door, wriggling across the screens greenly, investigating the mailbox.

In February and March most years, the City's Urban Forestry Branch sends people to test Winnipeg's remaining elms for Dutch elm disease, a fungal disease that arrived in Winnipeg in 1975. The fungi, dispersed by native elm bark beetles, blocks a tree's vascular system, preventing it from transporting sugars from the leaves to the roots and water from the roots to the leaves. The disease can also spread from tree to tree via their interconnected roots. There is no cure for DED: you can't amputate offending limbs in the hopes of saving the rest.

So I sit on the stairs with my rotten cervix, my sexually trans-mitted angst, and watch the tree move and not-move. We not-move together. I have watched the cats nibble on the crabgrass at the elm's base, chase the white moths the worms become in the dry grass at twilight. I have pulled insistent dandelions from amongst its surface roots. My neighbours mow my stretch of boulevard grass now without even asking when they do theirs, a shared obligation, the unsharp blades of my push mower clenched, silent as my rotten cervix. Once, a wheel fell off my push mower mid-push – a failed contraction, the labour nurse/my gas-powered neighbour muttering encouragement, insistent.

I will have to call to get my biopsy result today. I will also have to summon Urban Forestry technicians to stare up at a flagging branch, to decide whether the tree gets the neon orange dot of a DED diagnosis, of death, the hiss of the spray paint like an inadvertent intake of breath over the phone, the results in.

I don't know what to –

MY LADY PARTS hate me but the view from the sixth floor of the Manitoba Clinic – which houses neat rows of OB/GYNs, like rows of incubators in old-timey movies – saves me every time.

Heavy perimenopausal bleeding, almost hemorrhagic? Window. Fluid-filled cyst the size of a mandarin orange on an ovary? Window.

The view is all-gleaming asphalt and a rising river of old trees, swamping downtown. I am reassured that the city vanishes under the canopy in summer.

After dodgy Pap results, I am here for a colposcopy and somehow the window isn't enough of an intervention – I find myself pacing the pregnant hallway, walking my suspect cervix like a pissy dog on a leash. I stop and look down to the fifth-floor balcony, where the planters are filled with bamboo stakes and plastic owl facades, pointed in all the cardinal directions.

My cervix and I are amused by the hardcore pigeon deterrence and then I spot a plastic wolf the size of a late-summer zucchini tucked in amongst the bamboo, which looks to be half boar and, also, enraged about being so small.

For most of the spring and summer, I have been owl-watching in a cemetery, from an hour or so before sundown until it gets fully dark and the owls emerge from their snoozing roosts and begin their day. Mike and I go in the hopes of seeing the best bits of the great horned owl life cycle so I can write a book about it or maybe just a brochure. I have been admiring shed owl feathers but return them to the ground after I've photographed them, after I've turned them this way and that in what's left of the light, filled with admiration. Legally, you can't own owl feathers, but ejecta is another matter, so I have a Ziploc bag of owl pellets that I'm saving for winter like a taxidermist's Advent calendar. But I haven't owl-watched in weeks now and miss spending my Saturday nights sundowning with a great horned owl pair that refused to nest, this year's legacy only pellets and shed feathers. This year's activity was only me, watching owls fly away.

LYING ON THE exam table, I hear my gyne say, "The thing on my head is a microscope."

"I can't see you," I say, "but I believe you."

Today, Dr. Carrie Corbett is taking a tissue sample to test for cervical cancer. I busy myself visualizing dwarf wolves prowling windowsills instead of human papillomavirus (or HPV) lesions on my cervix. (I have already thoroughly visualized the lesions as black, like the lichen that specializes in rocky slopes in Shield country. My favourite thing in high summer when I was younger was the crunch when the dried-out lichen was stepped on . . .) This summer, I have a dwarf saskatoon manufacturing purple in a pot on my balcony. Maybe the wolf would feel drawn to it, feel a miniaturized kinship?

I say, out loud, that I once made out with a boy with cold sores.

"My tongue and gums got super swollen afterward," I elaborate. "I thought all my teeth were going to fall out."

Corbett says, "Um, that's herpes simplex virus," which, of

course, I knew. She mentions that she might perform a loop electrosurgical excision procedure (or LEEP) on my cervix later to remove the infected tissue. The brochure, tucked in my bag as I walk away from the building, also mentions cryosurgery, which I felt I should request on principle, so my cervix can be bionic or preserved in a vat next to Steve Jobs's head, never mind the cruelty of watery discharge for weeks.

These are the jokes I should have deployed in my gyne's office, like sexually transmitted infections, but instead I felt tired and sad and now I am trapped in my car by rain. For the first time in my life, I am thrilled when it rains.

Sitting there, I remember that when Corbett said, "Your cervix is shaped like a donut," I wanted to ask what kind.

If I could choose, I'd want my cervix to resemble a cruller.

COMING OUT IN the evening, looking for a moment of green transport – like a pelican's shadow at the river's edge, covering me entirely for a moment, like wading out in a lake and finally making it up to my armpits, my water-wing breasts vanishing under the swells – I spot instead the flagging leaves on a branch up high.

The branch is nearest the road, overhanging my dirty little Prius, the leaves obviously dry and crisp even from here. My stomach and my rotten cervix clench.

What could I have done to prevent this: Heat-wave watering? Preventative insecticide injections? Paying for treatment out of my rotten poetry budget? Or was it inevitable, an aging tree, an infected city and my hippy-dippy neighbourhood one of the hardest hit? Except this is not the urban forest, or an illustration of the three hundred thousand elms that have survived our civic imagination, our settler demands, it is my tree, my beloved, still strong but showing weakness seventy-five feet up – shrieking merlin height. Streetlamp height, even with dreadful full-moon LEDs. (Like a forehead microscope focused on my diseased lady parts, the light is unflinching.)

I have no symptoms, no phantom ache, but according to CancerCare I missed my Pap twice over, all the safeguards and bookkeeping failing me and my cervix. I should have known, somehow. Or I should have been out, merrily sharing my STI.

My gyne said HPV has been having a party on my cervix and here's me with anxiety that no one will show up at my book launches. Except I didn't have to send out a single invite. Corbett said it's proof that I had sex at some point in my life. Except the infection didn't resolve, like a twenty-year-old fling, like an old elm brooding over a trunk full of elm bark beetles, each of them wreathed with sticky fungal spores, anticipating a threesome with revving chainsaws.

Oh God. I hate waiting for test results. For authorities to tell you what's next, your diagnosis just another piece of paper in a file in a row of file cabinets. I want an elaborate chart of my sadness. Stage IV sadness – all over my flagging face and in my pants.

THAT NIGHT, WATCHING the rain pour down – a month's worth of rain in one day, like a basin that had been kicked over – I couldn't dredge up the energy to run to the house.

But I didn't want to sit in the car forever, so I opened the car door and took two steps and stood next to – and then leaned on – the trunk of my boulevard elm.

A mature elm might be umbrella-shaped, but it isn't an umbrella, so rain made its way through the branches, the flagging leaves, and landed on my head and shoulders. I was getting increasingly wet.

But the space under the branches, between my car and the

house, felt like a spare room someone I trusted was offering me. So I put my lined forehead against the rough trunk and focused on breathing, listening to the pelting rain and my breath.

I DON'T KNOW what to –

I don't know what to do with my climate-changed heat-stress, years of drought shelved alongside this year's heat dome. Instagram is all aluminum foil–covered windows, the forests to the east and west of us burning. The smoke hasn't drifted into town yet. The tree hasn't been condemned. But it's coming.

I dream of rain, scan the weather report full of headlines I don't want to read: extreme heat warnings, air quality warnings, empty farm dugouts, grasshopper infestations.

I haven't been dealing well with the heat. My house is not designed for weeks of high heat, rooms hot-air ballooning across airless afternoons. We retreat to our bedrooms, the window air conditioners/my mind whirring. We are heat-exhausted, hydro-affected, and I don't know what I'll do if my boulevard tree comes down.

What if the biggest loss in my life isn't my little granny, my divided father, his nose wandering across generations of angry women, but that elm? I would trade my mossy roof, my rotten cervix, for another leafy decade with that tree.

But maybe we don't get to choose. Maybe life isn't picking which catastrophe falls on your head like a dead branch, like a super-storm's worth of rain.

Maybe life is just standing as close as you can to a tree. Feeling connected to the world, for however long you've both got.

Fun Gal

MY FRIEND LAURA Lamont is fiercely intelligent and funny. She's a mycelial network, but instead of trees and plants, she connects and sustains people.

For years, Laura hosted a salon for women in her large house that was looked forward to with great anticipation by everyone who was lucky enough to get an invitation. Especially those of us with children: luxurious food and drink, prepared not-by-us! Time to eat/drink/chat with Laura's extended network of excellent women!

To have a thought and then another thought, uninterrupted!

For years, she made her family's cabin, an old farmhouse on the fringes of Riding Mountain National Park, available to me, because she knew I could use a place to write, to retreat to from the pressures of family life and work.

During the pandemic, early and late, Laura sent me flowers

virtually via Instagram Messenger every Friday. Pictures of glorious bouquets of flowers from all over the world. I don't even like cut flowers, but I liked these messages from Laura. They were cheering. They brought me into a community of excellent people, again, because I knew I wasn't the only one getting these Friday Flowers. (Recently, Mike and I were driving somewhere and he said, "Your friend Laura has been sending me flowers?" "Yah," I replied. "Isn't it great?")

Like Sue and Fiona Punter, the daughters of retired University of Manitoba botanist David Punter. I met one or both of them at Laura's salon back in the day. Laura told me that of late Sue and Fiona and Punter's wife, Elizabeth, had spent much of 2022 sorting, emptying and selling their house of forty years.

Around noon on March 31 – the day after my birthday – Laura sends me a photo of a stack of books about mushrooms. "Do you want any of these?" she asks.

"My temptation is to say that I'd take them all," I respond. "I don't want to be greedy and I'm not sure how much I'd consult them, but I love all things mushrooms, you know?"

"It's a giveaway, so you can have all of them," she says with the deep fatigue of someone helping to empty a house. "Saves someone packing them."

At 6:00 p.m., she messages again: "I have these for you."

"Wow," I respond. More books have been added to the original stack.

"You can sink into pages of fungi," Laura says. "They're just happy to have them go to a good home. You missed out on the eighty-year-old stuffed badger . . . went to another good home."

What's more, she said she was on her way over. Door-to-door service! What have I done to deserve such largesse?

"Anyway, happy mushroomy birthday!" she writes.

I'VE SPENT MOST of my adult life obsessed with mushrooms but most of the time I am the only one in my circle who cares about them. My life and my writing are devoted to showing people what is around them, drawing their attention to things they may not have noticed or spent very much time with.

Which is why I am so happy when my friends send me terrible photos of the mushrooms they found while on vacation or just on walks near their houses. It means that they've noticed mushrooms and, maybe, the other flora and fauna around them.

I am less happy when people send me pictures of the mushroomy shreds their dog has just eaten or the white mushroom growing in the plant they brought in from outside that has just dumped a bunch of white spores – "ARIEL IS THIS A DESTROY-ING ANGEL?!!?" – but that's because I am not enough of an expert to definitively ID half-eaten/smushed/badly-photographed mushrooms.

But people are sometimes less than enthusiastic about my enthusiasm for mushrooms.

In 2016, I was on a spring book tour to the northern community of Thompson, MB, with Anita Daher. We went to see the half-frozen Pisew Falls with our host, the painter and speech-language pathologist Louise Stewart-Bruneau. On the hike to and from the falls, I kept on finding mushrooms growing on trees. So I was constantly stopping and looking at, then photographing, the mushrooms. Which meant my pace wasn't the quickest.

Anita is funny and we have a relationship where we can be funny with each other. After the third or fourth or seventh stop, Anita started leaning her forehead on tree trunks while she waited, groaning.

"Look!" I said, showing Louise a particularly nice specimen.

"Let me guess," Anita moaned. "*Another mushroom.*"

FOR FORTY YEARS, David Punter led the majority of the mushroom walks and talks in the city.

In the late '70s, when I was a child, catching frogs and crayfish at our cabin in northwestern Ontario, listening to my mother read poems by Dennis Lee and Shel Silverstein, Punter was *the* Fun Guy.

From 1977 to 1979, for instance, he taught a University of Manitoba continuing education course called "Mushroom Identification":

A course for anyone wishing to learn the basic principles of identification of fleshy fungi, to enhance their ability to gather and enjoy wild mushrooms. There will be three lecture sessions in an informal laboratory setting. The first two sessions will provide a brief description of the biology of fleshy fungi, including their life forms, their internal organization, their importance in the living world and their uses and dangers for man. Particular emphasis will be given to those characteristics which are most useful in classification and identification. Books, reference material, and identification manuals will be discussed. The first week will conclude with a Saturday morning foray followed by an afternoon in the laboratory to name the collections. In the final session we will delve into some of the techniques for microscopic examination of mushrooms. We will also consider the basis for some practical problems in mushroom identification and what can be done to alleviate these problems. The course will end with a second foray and identification session.

These workshops were in addition to his duties as a professor, which included teaching courses but also research and community service. His research focused on "the reproductive biology and population genetics of dwarf mistletoe and pathology, ecology and taxonomy of fungi associated with wild rice."

His community service was sitting on committees but also answering questions from the public about plants and fungi, responding to envelopes bulging with brittle leaves or softening mushrooms.

August 26, 1974
Dept. of Agriculture, U. of Manitoba

Dear Sir,
We appreciate if you can identify the mushroom we enclosed which we found abundantly in our backyard. Please give us the information whether it is poisonous or edible and under what kind of condition it grows, if undesirable, how to get rid of it. Thank you in anticipation for your help.

Yours truly, Mrs. E. Chung
Stalker Bay, Winnipeg

September 4, 1974
Dear Mrs. Chung,
Your mushroom has been passed to me by the Plant Science Department for identification. As far as I can determine from the dried specimen, it is *Marasmius oreades*, a fungus that is commonly found in lawns and grassy places. This species is edible, indeed it is one of our best wild mushrooms. It may also be kept for long periods without deterioration if it is air dried. *M. oreades* also may cause fairy rings in lawns; however the effects of these are usually not severe and may be minimized by adequate fertilizing and watering. If you wish to eat your mushrooms, I suggest that

you bring in a few fresh specimens so that I may confirm the identification. Alternatively, try a small quantity and if you develop no untoward symptoms within a thirty-six-hour period you may consider them safe. This procedure is always a wise precaution when eating unfamiliar mushrooms as certain individuals may produce an allergic reaction to species that are generally considered edible. Let me know if I can be of further assistance.

Yours sincerely,
D. Punter, Professor

FOR TEN YEARS, Punter had an office down the hall from me.

My office was between the elevator and a hallway that had bathrooms to one side and the entrance to the St. John's College Library at the end. It was on the third floor of the college, which had the library and a cluster of offices but no classrooms.

It was perfect. My office was an addition after the elevator was added, so I had a breath of separation from my colleagues down the hall. One wall was entirely windows and the rest were filled with my desk and bookshelves. For me, shelves were for the books I worked on for the press but also for filling with the rocks/nuts/mushrooms/feathers/bits of wood I collected in the nearby Southwood Lands. The windowsills were for potted plant cuttings from the Buller Greenhouse, two buildings over, which allowed visitors one plant per visit.

Between my colleagues' offices down the hall and mine were the retired fellow offices. That was where the college put retired academics who'd had offices in the building and who still wanted to maintain an office outside their homes. These profs were a valuable part of college life – they attended lectures and other college events and often advised younger profs – but I used to joke that they were stacked like cordwood in the retired fellows' offices.

As someone who shared a wall with one bank of these offices, I was party to one retired prof who regularly yelled at Skype, the pre-pandemic video-calling software. He wasn't angry, he was just calling elderly colleagues/friends/family and one or both of them hadn't figured out how to adjust the volume on their computer or were hard of hearing.

One advantage was that these profs, who'd been forcibly downsized after twenty or thirty years to one or two shelves of books instead of an entire office's worth, often jettisoned books when they moved into the retired fellows' offices. Stacks of books would appear on a designated table mid-hallway. Though the research these books contained was dated, there were sometimes gems, with beautiful paper and binding, with colour plates, or early editions of classics.

David Carr, my boss and the director of University of Manitoba Press at the time, kept an eye on the table. He'd take books for his large extended family or bring me ones he thought I would find interesting, if I'd missed them. He would also quietly put unclaimed books in the large blue recycle bins at the end of the hallway if they'd been on the table more than a week. He did it with a certain amount of relish, knowing that I was always faintly scandalized by the throwing-away of books.

My favourite thing about that hallway, besides the breath of separation it afforded me, besides the cast-off books, was that the recycle bin had "No Hot Ashes" imprinted on it. These bins were a remnant from an earlier era at the university, when everyone smoked and had ashtrays full of ashes to dispose of. A part of me likes to imagine hallway recycling-bin fires, drafts of academic papers and old books turning into ash themselves.

THE OLDEST BOOK in the stack of David Punter's books is *Mushrooms and Toadstools* (1954) by John Ramsbottom. "PUNTER" is scrawled in blue ink inside the front cover, which also contains an undated newspaper clipping, ripped/cut out in a hurry, of an illustrated column called *CHILDREN: Up and Doing by Peter Briton*. This edition was entitled "Woodland Danger": "You may hate them – but most people eat one of them. And another gave us penicillin. So on your next walk through the woods, when you're tired of kicking up dead leaves, try to spot some of these curious plants called 'fungi.'"

About halfway through the book, I find a mimeographed note on a half sheet of paper: "Research Students' Group Photograph A group photograph will be taken in front of the Botany School at 2:15 p.m. on Tuesday, 16 May. All Research Students are asked to be there punctually at that time. K.R. Sporne. 13 May, 1961." In the top left corner in blue ink: "Mr. Punter." On the back, in black ink, a list of mushrooms, using their Latin names. Three names have question marks next to them.

A quick Internet search reveals that Kenneth Robert Sporne (1915–89) was a British botanist and plant morphologist who lectured at Cambridge University. Comparing that to the official bio that accompanies Punter's fonds at the UM Archives and Special Collections, I see that he got a BA in Natural Science (Honours Botany) in 1959 and a PhD in Forest Pathology in 1964, both from Cambridge. The Ramsbottom was likely a textbook for him, something he often consulted.

Next is *Twenty Common Mushrooms: And How to Cook Them* (1965) by George S. Collins (Identification), Catherine R. Hammond (Drawings) and Margaret H. Lewis (Cookery). "To Mel Staves Best Wishes George S. Coffin" in blue ink inside. Which means that this book has already passed through another set of hands before it got to Punter.

By the time *The Club and Coral Mushrooms (Clavarias) of the United States and Canada* by William Chambers Coker came out in 1974, Punter had been appointed as Assistant Professor in the Botany Department at UM. The book has DAVID PUNTER stamped in blue ink inside and a price tag on the front from UManitoba bookstore: $5.95.

Then two books by Richard and Karen Haard. *Poisonous & Hallucinogenic Mushrooms* (1975), has DAVID PUNTER stamped in blue ink inside. There's a price tag on the front from the UManitoba bookstore: $3.95. *Foraging for Edible Wild Mushrooms* (1978) is unmarked. Finally, there are *Collins Guide to Mushrooms & Toadstools* (1978) by Morten Lange & F. Bayard Hora, with DAVID PUNTER stamped in blue ink inside, and *Edible Mushrooms* (1981) by Clyde M. Christensen, with a price tag on the back: $13.50.

[undated]
Dear Sir:
Will you please examine these mushrooms and tell me if they are edible or poisonous. They grew on an island in Lake of Woods. Some are reddish on top the others are brown or tan and really more plentiful. Have you any literature on mushrooms that we could have? Is it true that if a mushroom can be peeled easily it is edible?

Thank you, B. Kilpatrick
Banting Drive, Winnipeg

August 1, 1975
Dear Ms Kilpatrick,
Your mushrooms arrived today in semi-liquid state, beyond all hope of identification. At this time of year, it is best to bring them

here directly or allow them to dry before mailing; their useful life when in a plastic bag at high temperatures is very short. As far as literature is concerned I would recommend a pamphlet entitled *Mushroom Collecting for Beginners* and a book *Edible and Poisonous Mushrooms of Canada* both by Groves and obtainable from the Information Canada bookstore on Portage Avenue. There is no truth to the suggestion that easily peelable mushrooms are edible – some of the most dangerous ones peel well. I fear there is one simple rule for telling the edible from the poisonous. The old story about blackening silver spoons is equally unreliable as a test.

Yours sincerely, D. Punter, Associate Professor

WHEN I WAS a teenager in the late '80s, rowing on the Red and Assiniboine Rivers, when I was specializing in fries with gravy and root beer Slurpees, Punter was *the* Fun Guy.

Punter taught a course in 1982, 1984 and 1985 called "Mushrooms and Their Relatives" for the Fort Whyte Centre for Environmental Education: "Food, friend, or foe? Fungi affect us all in one way or another, and Dr. David Punter, of the Dept. of Botany, University of Manitoba, returns to present his popular introduction to these plants without leaves, flowers, stems, or roots. Field trip in the afternoon, and workshop, slides, and perhaps some sampling in the evening."

Between 1986 and 1988 he taught a similar class called "Mushrooms and Other Fungi" at Fort Whyte.

IN 2021, MY daughter, Anna, fell in love with the TV show *Succession*. She finds it endlessly interesting. She wants to watch/make fan edits or read fan fiction or participate in the fandom online all the time. I find the show itself nasty and brutish but, sadly, not short, so I have so far refused to watch any more after the pilot. But she still talks to me about it nearly every day, showing me the media she is consuming.

But that's not all: after a decade of being hauled along on walks in the woods, after ten years – more than half her life – of peering at mushrooms with me, she's declared that she's "not outdoorsy." She doesn't want to go for walks with me in the woods anymore, though she describes her aesthetic as "cottagecore" and so appreciates the whole mulchy palette.

I figure Anna's owed some time that's not about what I like. So even though I've only watched the first episode and she's three seasons in – and avidly and eagerly awaiting the launch of the fourth season – I'm almost what you'd call a subject area expert from listening to her.

Anna says that my favourite shows all involve mean old women. And she's not wrong: I love *Vera* and *The Closer*, both of which feature smart canny women who are pitbulls when it comes to solving crimes. Which is to say: they take hold of ideas and shake them to death.

Sometimes, Anna admits that she wishes she had someone to talk to about *Succession* (or her long-term love, *Doctor Who* . . .) that loves it as much as she does.

I know exactly what she means: I've always wanted someone to talk mushrooms with. A mushroom kindred spirit.

That is possibly a mean old woman.

DAVID PUNTER RETIRED in 2006. That year is outlined in gold for me because that's the year that Anna was born, when I poured her into baby-holding contraptions and took her for walks in the Assiniboine Forest, bending carefully, awkwardly, to look at mushrooms. I felt scraped raw, strong and weak all at once, but I was determined to keep doing what I loved.

I didn't start working at the University of Manitoba Press until 2011 and my first impressions of Punter were that he was tall and thin with an admirable white beard. He was soft-spoken and had retained his British accent, even after more than fifty years in Canada.

Besides the fact that Punter was one of two bearded retired profs who wore shorts, showing off their knobby knees, he was in all other respects proper. Reserved.

I am not. I laugh too loudly. Worse, I laugh at my own jokes. My favourite thing is people who laugh heartily at my jokes too, like the historian/UM librarian Jim Blanchard, like David Carr. When Jim Blanchard died in late 2022, I realized that most of my memories of him were standing at the back of book launches, laughing and gossiping. In the last years of his life, I didn't see Jim much, mostly because of the pandemic, but I always meant to get in touch, to ask if he wanted to go for a walk.

In the last years of my time at UMP, I always meant to befriend Punter, to turn him into my mushroom mentor.

But we always seemed to miss each other. It seemed to me that the gulf between our personalities, our educations and maybe even our generations was too great.

June 14, 1978
D. Punter, University of Man
I would like these species analyzed for edible quality. Please send report on them, and if these are morels. Thank you.

Yours truly, Peter Proskie
Lynn Lake, Manitoba

June 21, 1978

Dear Mr. Proskie:

Your fungus specimens were not in the best of condition after their journey, but I have been able to make an identification for you. They are False Morels of the genus *Gyromitra*. The mycologists are not in full agreement over the classification of this group but I suspect it would be safe to call your fungus *G. esculenta (Pers.) Fries*. In any case it should not be eaten as most members of this group contain toxic substances which are only partially removed by boiling. I hope this is the information you need.

Yours sincerely, D. Punter, Associate Professor

ONCE, WALKING BETWEEN UMP's main office and my office I spied a stack of mushroom books on the giveaway table. I scooped them up, jubilant, knowing they were likely David Punter's castoffs.

The next time I saw Punter in the hallway, I stopped to tell him how much I appreciated the books.

"I hadn't actually put them out on the giveaway table. That was my colleague," he said, dryly.

It was the Skype Shouter! I should have known.

"I have them right here!" I yelped. "I'll get them right now!"

I ran back to my office and retrieved the stack, which I hadn't yet brought home, thinking I'd dip into them on my lunch hours.

Except for one: *Mr Jackson's Mushrooms* by H.A.C. Jackson (1877–1961), an exhibition catalogue published in 1979 by the National Gallery of Canada. It was the size of a large children's picture book, full of Jackson's beautiful botanical illustrations of mushrooms and a diary of his mushroom hunts from 1931 to 1954. Talent ran in the family apparently: Jackson's younger brother was A.Y. Jackson, a member of the Group of Seven.

As I handed Punter the stack of books, I explained that I had one book at home but that I'd bring it back the next week.

Except . . . I didn't. I was entranced by the diaries, by the paintings of mushrooms. They seemed to glow. I had the idea of combining my mushroom diary, my macro photographs of mushrooms, with his as though it was a correspondence between us.

Punter never brought it up, in all the times I saw him after that in the hallways or at lunchtime lectures, as we separately slurped our soup.

WHEN I WAS an adult and walking in Winnipeg's Assiniboine Forest regularly, just starting to notice mushrooms, when I was hauling Anna in a sled, Punter was still *the* Fun Guy.

The last notice I find for one of his workshops is 2019, "Morels & Other Fungi," through Nature Manitoba at Kelvin High School: "Morels are the mushrooms that appear in the spring while most other fungi can be found in late August and September. Participants in this workshop will begin learning to identify mushrooms in time for the morel season."

Punter offered this workshop every year from 2011 to 2019. Kelvin is, of course, the school my daughter began to attend in 2020.

I somehow never took one of his classes. I was too young or too busy with friends and school and first jobs or out of the city, attending journalism school. Busy with child-rearing. It was always something.

IN DECEMBER 2022, it takes me two hours to find *Mr Jackson's Mushrooms*. I look for it in every room in the house, which is to say, every room where there are stacks of books.

It has been a couple of years since I examined it closely. And I am entranced all over again, the text and images telling me so much about H.A.C. Jackson. In my mushroom-book hunt, I also find an ex–Winnipeg Public Library copy of *Edible and Poisonous Mushrooms of Canada* (1979) by J. Walton Groves, which Punter often recommended in his letters. And of course it has a frontispiece by H.A.C. Jackson, of incandescent *Amanita caesarea*. Groves had good access to Jackson's work, having married Jackson's eldest daughter, Naomi. Like her father and uncle, Naomi was a painter in addition to her day job as an art historian who received her PhD from Harvard.

Punter would have been almost two years old, Naomi twenty-eight and me minus thirty-five when Jackson wrote this 1938 account of a trip to his local, the La Salle Woods:

A red-letter day or rather a red-letter night. Made up my mind that I would be on the spot this year lest my unknown competitor get ahead of me. Last year, not a single *Morchella esculenta* was seen at the stand in the La Salle Woods. At the time I blamed the weather but now it is hard to believe in the light of tonight's collecting that not a specimen should have appeared. The Woods were still and quiet; no human being except myself in the region. The fresh green of the young foliage and myriads of spring flowers made an appealing setting. Yes and voracious mosquitoes were there to take the edge off my pleasure. On the way to the Morel ground I scattered the specimens of Gyromitra collected at Chambly in the hopes they might establish themselves in the neighbourhood. Came at last to the spot and there right in my gaze was a beautiful *Morchella esculenta* almost orange in colour, then another and another. I decided to make a careful census and counted 19 mature specimens, mostly at the lower end of the station. Took nine and covered most of the others with leaves lest they be too conspicuous. Well, this has been a satisfactory year for Morels. Three varieties as well as *Gyromitra esculenta* and another splendid location established behind St. Lambert. Came home feeling very happy and contented indeed.

DAVID PUNTER AND I only had one other conversation that I remember.

I had been regularly walking the Southwood Lands, between University Crescent and Pembina Highway ever since the university had bought the land that the Southwood Golf Course had occupied.

The Southwood Lands were bisected by a gravelly road and it had the only free parking within kilometres of the university. I was reluctant to spend eleven dollars for a day's parking, so on the days I wasn't carpooling I would walk, either from gravel Markham or beyond when that was full. It was a half-hour of walking, into and through the decommissioned golf course, which was slated for all kinds of development but that mostly sat fallow for the time I walked there.

I am all about passive use. And free parking.

But when the plans for Southwood's development came out and were posted on campus for the public to see, I went to visit, peering at the various architects' drawings of a future Southwood with a feeling of dread. None of the architects had walked there. None of them had eaten its deep red crabapples or berthed the hordes of geese, snatched glimpses of raptors on snags or jackrabbits bounding through the long grasses. None of them had collected elm oysters from the growing pile of stumps or palmed a dud goose egg, watching creatures come and go over the seasons, live and die.

I approached a biologist to go for a walk in Southwood and he suggested that we bring David, who was clearly someone he admired, both in how he wrote about him in his emails and how he addressed David during the walk. It was an outing that took many emails to arrange.

I was (and am) an email hoarder. I deleted spam and the bureaucratic emails the university would regularly send, but I kept most everything else. It was a personal archive, a proof of concept. But I was forced by another bureaucratic email to delete a chunk of my work emails, so I don't recall who the biologist was or what his connection was to Southwood. There must have been one, but the email is gone and my memory of the email is gone too. What I do remember is that David peered at and spoke about the various non-native ornamental trees that had been planted at some point by Southwood groundskeepers.

It had been a dry season, so there weren't very many mushrooms to look at. But I managed to find one in a small beard of trees and handed it to him – like it was a piece of heirloom jewellery, like it was a egg or a baby chick, impossibly small and fragile – before I'd even had a look myself. He looked at it, said something I didn't catch – probably its Latin name, which I am admittedly bad at retaining – then threw it over his shoulder. Like he had spilled salt, that same sort of superstitious élan.

NEXT IN THE stack of books is *Mushrooms of Northwest North America* (1991) by Helene M.E. Schalkwijk-Barendsen. There's a gold return address sticker inside, reading R. Krahn, Bluewater Crescent. It is annotated throughout in pencil, with checkmarks next to images/text and locations where they were found: "White Lake Sept 21" next to *Leccinum snellii* and "Rough stalk" next to *Leccinum boreale*. But it's hard to know if these are Punter's or Krahn's notes. It's hard to know if this book was borrowed and never returned, if Krahn was a friend.

Given that I never returned *Mr Jackson's Mushrooms*, this is a satisfying find. It makes me feel less guilty, but part of me wonders: Would *Mr Jackson's Mushrooms* have been in the stack if I had returned it? Would I have been the inheritor of this book anyway?

Next on the stack is *Children and Toxic Fungi: The essential medical guide to fungal poisoning in children* (1995) by Roy Watling. Given its grim contents, this a slim book, dwarfed by the other tomes. It has DAVID PUNTER stamped in blue ink inside and a price tag on the back from Royal Botanic Garden Edinburgh: £10.00. *Mushrooms of Ontario and Eastern Canada* (1999) by George Barron also has DAVID PUNTER stamped inside, but this time he used black ink.

In this era, Punter was Head of the Department of Botany. He also acted as a forensics expert in criminal court cases and consulted with poison control at the Health Science Centre.

September 27, 1987
Dear Dr. Punter
You might recall I came to see you about identifying a species of wild mushroom. We both agreed it is a species of Armillaria which is recommended edible. Well . . . we ate it, by that I mean three of us (my husband, my elder son & myself) & got sick over it, and my younger son (who is quite picky about "new" things) didn't get sick. While I well remember that it could be due to each individual's level of tolerance to food stuff, I feel it is my responsibility to inform you that this event did happen for fear of the possibility of similar unfortunate events taking place. Please feel free to contact me if you have any further questions. I remain,

Yours sincerely, Lucia P. Ellis.
Woodlawn Ave, Winnipeg

[no reply]

ON A SUNDAY in November 2022, I come out to find a large brown envelope in my mailbox that holds various items of mushroom kitsch, including a tea towel, paper napkins and a stack of mushroom greeting cards and postcards.

There is no warning text message and no note, but the envelope was originally addressed to Laura Lamont, so I know this is more of David Punter's stuff.

The napkins, highly decorated and stiff, function terribly as napkins. It's like ripping a page out of a children's book and trying to wipe your face with it. But they look nice on a table. I can just see David's smile drooping as he opened the present this came in. Because: decorative/useless napkins. But also because they depict a cluster of *Amanita muscaria*, otherwise known as fly agaric, which is pretty, common and toxic. Who wants to wipe their face with a mushroom you wouldn't want to eat, unless you were looking for a big hallucinogenic-laden ride?

I decide that I will unfold and use them as tissue in gifts, then set them aside.

I spend more time with the cards, about half of which feature illustrations by Beatrix Potter. One of the Internet things that people share with me over and over are Beatrix Potter's mushroom botanical drawings: "Have you seen this?"

Potter is best known for her Tales, stories for children that she wrote and illustrated herself, starting in 1901 when she self-published *The Tale of Peter Rabbit*. It was commercially published in 1902 to great success and in 1903, Peter Rabbit was released as a stuffie. He was, in fact, the first licensed character to be released as a toy. Potter was also well known for her sheep breeding and farming, as well as her land conservation. She was also a respected mycologist, painting whole mushrooms as well as microscopic drawings of fungus spores, specifically of the agarics. Potter even submitted a paper, "On the Germination of the Spores of the

Agaricineae," to the Linnean Society in 1897. Of course she wasn't encouraged by the other male mycologists or allowed to attend the meeting to hear her paper read. Her paper looked specifically at *Flammulina velutipes* or the velvet foot, one of my favourite mushrooms.

This is the first time I've had any of her work in my hands that I could study closely. There are two sizes of postcards of her work in this little packet. Each one has the species name, then a blanket statement: "One of a large collection of watercolours given to the Armitt Library by the artist herself; an early member and benefactor. Sold in aid of the Armitt Trust. [copyright] ARMITT TRUST, Ambleside, Cumbria."

There are also a series of blank greeting cards with envelopes from the British Mycological Society with paintings by R.E. Cowell, circa 1982. Cowell is hard to find online, but he is described as the "British mycogastronomist and painter" in the April 1977 edition of *Spore Prints*, the bulletin of the Puget Sound Mycological Society. My favourite of Cowell's artworks is the "*Flammulina velutipes*. Winter Fungus or Velvet Shank. 2/3 actual size," which shows a cluster of this mushroom growing through the bark of a tree branch like the claws of a tiger tattoo through a thigh.

Of the two, I prefer Beatrix Potter's version, though I'd be happy to look at either every day, on my wall or on the boulevard, growing out of an elm stump.

There's also a set of shrink-wrapped British Mycological Society picture postcards and a few loose ones, which shows that they were used, at least. Finally, there's a little packet of picture postcards by Tessa Traeger, copyrighted to 1994.

I start to make lists in my head of who I could send these to. But realize that I'd have to text the majority of the people I'd like to send them to, to ask for their addresses.

A part of me wants to treat them like tarot cards: a pretty deck of images that helps me to reconnect with myself.

THERE ARE TWO post-retirement books on the pile.

Tricholomas of North America: A Mushroom Field Guide (2013) by Alan and Arleen Bessette and two others is published by University of Texas Press. It has no markings, no stamps or price tags.

The last one was probably sent to Punter as a gift during the pandemic, as it is the UK edition: *Entangled Life: How Fungi Make Our Worlds, Change Our Minds and Shape Our Futures* (2020) by Merlin Sheldrake. Sheldrake's dedication isn't to his "parapsychologist" father, Rupert, or his "musical visionary" brother Cosmo, but to his subject: "With gratitude to the fungi from which I have learned."

And that's it: an entire career in books. A life amongst mushrooms.

IT IS THE very end of 2022 when I visit Laura Lamont's house for the first time in years. Laura Lamont's niece Jamie is studying entomology at the University of Manitoba and wants to show me their nature journals, full of writing and drawings.

We drink strong tea and nibble on year-end baking from the Lilac Bakery.

It is exactly what I need. Tea! Imperial cookies! Kindred-spirit conversation! But before I can leave, there are still two things left to do. First, Laura has to go upstairs and select a small stack of Terry Pratchett novels from her shelves for me, perfect for light midwinter reading.

Second, she has to carefully measure out four cups of wild rice from an enormous sack into a brown paper lunch bag. This is David Punter's wild rice; he was apparently a huge'wild rice fan aside from it being a research interest. Laura is, of course, determined to eat her way through the entire bag but is also giving some away.

Later, I learn that Jamie has wound up with Punter's much-thumbed copy of *Edible and Poisonous Mushrooms of Canada* as well as a much older book, *The Fungi of Manitoba* (1929) by G.R. Bisby, A.H. Reginald Buller and John Dearness.

Of course, I have the University of Manitoba library copy of *The Fungi of Manitoba* on my desk as I write. Generations and generations!

September 28, 1992

Dr. Punter

Could you please identify this mushroom for me? It was picked 1 week ago at Falcon Lake at the base of a birch tree. I froze 3 margarine containers but did not eat any. We met about 6 weeks ago at your home I dropped by with *Armillaria mellea*, which is plentiful at Falcon Lake now. Could you please call me at home or at work. I appreciate this very much.

Bernice Diamond
Northumbria Bay, Winnipeg

Cortinarius sp. Phoned 2/10. DP.

I HAVE TO say: I love this inheritance of mushrooms.

Too often, people spend a whole life collecting pins or figurines or vases or shoes, becoming an expert in enamel or bisque figurines or UV glass or chunky heels. Their spouses/children aren't usually as avid as they are and, most of the time, have no idea what the collection is worth or who might want it or how best to sell it when the collector is gone. Sometimes, those collections are dumped at thrift stores. Other times, I suspect they go straight in the dumpster. Profs often face similar problems when they come to the end of their careers. Who wants their books/academic journals/research papers? Where will they put what they decide to keep? It's a massive job, much like downsizing a family home.

I am glad that Laura had a mushroom-mad friend for Punter's daughters to direct some of his mushroom books and ephemera to.

But I think that's how knowledge transfer works. It isn't always direct. It can be affected by personality or even happenstance.

In the end, I learned about mushrooms by walking in the forest, by slowly getting to know different species. I learned about them from books, from field guides, written by generations of people who loved mushrooms as much as I did. Slowly, I've become a Fun Gal.

I know that walking in the woods was part of how Punter, Winnipeg's Fun Guy, learned too. I know that he took this knowledge and broadcast it widely, to generations of Winnipeggers, like a mushroom releasing spores, hoping it would land on fertile ground.

I may not have benefitted from David Punter's knowledge formally, but sitting in the university archives, hearing his voice as I read his letters to ordinary people who were curious enough about mushrooms to send a letter, sitting at my desk, reading the books he valued enough to stamp with his name, is more than enough for me.

Pidpanky Picker

IN LATE SEPTEMBER 2023, it started.

Endless notifications on my phone: "Do these look like honey mushrooms? i brought the cluster home to do a spore print as well but i was wondering if anyone has any ideas!"

Endless notifications on my laptop: "Pretty sure these are honey mushrooms, but still want to do my due diligence."

Even notifications in my dreams: "Help, is this honey mushroom, spore print is white . . ."

"It started," of course, means both the flush of honey mushooms, *Armillaria* spp, in stands of trees across Manitoba and people posting to the Winnipeg Mycological Society/Société mycologique de Winnipeg group on Facebook.

After twenty years of looking at mushrooms by myself, learning them slowly over many walks under trees, I've found myself in a communal mushroom space. There were people who knew far more about mushrooms than me and people who knew far less. Not only that, I was suddenly being informed when, if not where, choice edibles like morels, chanterelles, oysters and honey mushrooms were appearing out in the world.

I also realized that while I was an expert on the mushrooms that appeared in Assiniboine Forest, in aspen-oak parkland, I had monocultured my mushroom knowledge, because mushrooms grow in all kinds of environments.

A few years ago, based on advice from the WMS, I started foraging for morels in the spring. It was a strange and rocky undertaking but it also resulted in a few glorious mouthfuls, full of umami: buttery garlicky morels on toast, morels swimming in soup.

But this fall, it felt like everyone was muttering directly into my ear about honey mushrooms: "I've had the best crop ever of honey mushrooms in my yard!"; "Honey mushrooms for days!!"; "The biggest padpanki, aka honey mushroom, that I have ever seen and not infested!"

They meant infested by insects of all grades and descriptions. Also slugs and worms. Fungi are part of an ecosystem, which means they're part of a web that connects them to the flora and fauna around them. They eat and are eaten.

But those exclamations and celebrations also came with warnings: "This is a reminder that honey mushrooms are not a beginner mushroom to forage and eat," and "Here are some examples of some lookalikes growing in amongst honey mushroom clusters."

Those look-alikes – which are toxic to humans if they're ingested – include shaggy scalycaps (*Pholiota squarrosa*), sulfur tufts (*Hypholoma fasciculare*) and jack-o'lanterns (*Omphalotus illudens*).

ALEXANDRE BRASSARD, THE founder and majordomo of the WMS, commented on the mega-flush on October 2: "We seem to hit a record for honey mushrooms (*Armillaria*) foraging this year. Congrats to the lucky ones! We've had a very dry and hot summer, which can be stressful for trees and make them more suceptible to *Armillaria* root infection. I wonder if that explains the bumper crop. Just a wild guess."

The year 2023 had been a strange and climate-changed one. According to Environment and Climate Change Canada's chief climatologist David Phillips when he appeared on CBC Manitoba to talk about his year-end Top 10 weather stories, March and April had been exceptionally cold.

"There wasn't a melting temperature in Winnipeg in all of March – morning, noon and night it was below freezing and that has never happened in a hundred and fifty years. And then May and June came and my gosh, spring lasted two days – it went from winter to summer!"

May and June were the warmest on record, but somehow Manitoba was one of the few provinces that escaped the endless summer of rural wildfires and wildfire smoke that was blowing into the urban centres.

"Both July and August were cooler than normal followed by a very warm September, making for a relatively long summer and one of the longest growing seasons on record."

One result of this particular set of conditions, apparently, was that the woods were chockablock with honey mushrooms, which are tree parasites. Meaning: they injure or kill trees. Just as climate change makes forest fires burn hotter and longer, it also provides conditions for parasites like *Armillaria* to thrive.

By mid-afternoon on Friday, October 6, I was feeling positively itchy wanting to go get me some honeys, but I knew I would need some help finding and definitively identifying them. So I texted

Tom Nagy – who, in addition to being knowledgeable about grow-ing mushrooms indoors, is also skilled at foraging for them – to ask if he had time to go mushrooming with me.

He got back to me the next morning, saying that on Sunday we could go to Birds Hill Provincial Park, forty minutes from the city, where the Winnipeg Folk Festival is held each summer. I have been to the festival any number of times, but I have almost never gone for a hike there. It always struck me as being similar to Assiniboine Forest but with more roads. Which is to say, a degraded woods.

Tom picked me up early-ish Sunday morning in his Peg City Car Co-op vehicle.

By mid-afternoon, we were driving back, laden with honeys.

LIKE ME, ALEXANDRE Brassard taught himself about mushrooms.

"I regularly encountered mushrooms as a kid, while walking around my parents' cottage in the Lac Saint-Jean region, in Qué-bec. It was teeming with brightly coloured *Russula* and *Suillus*, which were fascinating but also taboo, as I was sternly warned not to touch any wild mushroom. Oh, the frisson of the forbidden fungus!"

Brassard characterizes his parents as foodies, saying that they enjoyed eating wild mushrooms in restaurants but weren't interested in foraging themselves. Though early on their impulse was to warn him off picking wild, possibly poisonous mushrooms, when they saw his interest continue into his teen years, they encouraged him.

My high school also had a forest trail where my best friend and I found a few morels. It was to identify those speci-mens that I read my first field guide, and that's how I got hooked. We took part in a science fair where we com-puterized dichotomous identification keys on a shiny new Commodore 64. We were sent to the fair's provincial finals, and I even gave a lecture at the local mushroom club. Since then, I never stopped studying and picking mushrooms, although it was more complicated when I moved to Toronto for my doctoral training.

The most important gift his parents gave him was a copy of René Pomerleau's *Flore des Champignons au Québec*, which Brassard says is still one of the greatest North American mycological resources. "That book taught me so much. Then I started reading biology sources like Bryce Kendrick's *The Fifth Kingdom*, and searching scientific articles to answer more specific questions. Later, biology professor Sylvie Rondeau taught me basic lab and microscopy techniques – she was very patient – and I read a few lab manuals to develop my own protocols in order to collect specimens, curate a fungarium, grow mycelium in petri dishes, cultivate mushrooms on various substrates and conduct fun little experiments."

Though Brassard is passionate about fungi, his training is as a political science prof. He now teaches both subjects at the Université de Saint-Boniface, Winnipeg's French-language university.

When I moved to Manitoba, eight years ago, I was delighted that Winnipeg is close to a variety of beautiful forest habitats: oak groves, aspen parkland, pine stands, river bottom elms and box elders, boreal mixed forest, all within a short driving distance. I was quite excited to explore Manitoba's mushroom species. I don't know local traditions very well, but a few Franco-Manitoban friends told me about their family morels and chanterelles picking spots near Marchand or Victoria Beach. I didn't torture them enough to find out their secret spots, though. A Métis colleague also mentioned his forays and I'd love to do ethnomycological field work with Métis elders, some day.

Brassard, who came to Manitoba to take the dual roles of Dean of the Faculty of Arts and of the Faculty of Science at USB, appreciates how these concurrent roles allow him to formally connect political science and fungi.

In 2019, he founded the Winnipeg Mycological Society/Société mycologique de Winnipeg group on Facebook: "I was about to teach the introductory mycology course and labs at Université de Saint-Boniface, but most field references were from Québec, Ontario, British Columbia, so I wanted to get a general sense of the local fungal diversity. What species are common in Manitoba? When do they fructify? In what part of the province?"

Though he used the group as a place to post his photos, other people found the page and started posting their own photos, asking for help with identification, so he started to help them and other experienced foragers joined in. The page now has more than 9,600 followers, many of whom are asking that Brassard organize forays, workshops and cooking classes.

And so, as the honeys flushed out in the woods, Brassard incorporated the WMS as a not-for-profit organization.

"Next steps? A first general assembly to adopt the bylaws, elect the WMS officers, recruit volunteers and decide together which activities and events we want to carry out. If all goes well, we should be able to register members soon. I'm preparing an online course on mushroom ID and it would be great to organize a first guided foray next spring, just in time for morel season."

Brassard's "foray" into mushroom organizing has broadened his understanding not only of mushrooms but the people who love them: "This little adventure is teaching me that people are very curious about mushrooms, and that fungi can appeal to them in a variety of ways. For some it's the culinary aspect, other are into life science, ecology, or hiking, some are nature photographers, a few like ID 'detective work,' make crafts, or enjoy cultivating oyster mushrooms in their backyard. Some people seek psychedelic experiences or swear by the alleged medicinal properties of chaga. Fungi have something for everyone."

DONNA KORMILO WAS another person intently watching the posts on the WMS about honey mushrooms.

All four of her grandparents immigrated to Canada from western Ukraine, in the Ternopil region, in the early 1900s. All four families brought with them the tradition of picking mushrooms, specifically honey mushrooms, which, depending on how the Ukrainian Cyrillic alphabet was romanized, are called pidpenky or pidpanky or even padpanki.

In 1960, when Donna was five years old and in half-day kindergarten, she remembers being picked up by her mother, Olga Basisty Kormilo, in the fall and being taken to harvest honey mushrooms.

"She knew how to drive so in the afternoon we'd go to the Argyle area, to small cattle pastures with oak trees," Donna said. "I learned how to walk carefully to avoid stepping into cow pies or mushrooms."

"Eating pidpanky has always been part of our meatless December 24, Christmas Eve, meal," Donna continued. "Frozen, thawed, fried with finely diced onions and whipping cream added. Not totally meatless as frying in butter and adding cream, some would argue, defeats the purpose. Tradition would have sauce made with browned flour and water."

People of Eastern European extraction observing the Orthodox religious calendar don't celebrate Christmas until January 7.

Christmas Eve dinner, falling on January 6, is an important part of that tradition. Though in places where the dominant culture says that Christmas is on December 25, some members of the Ukrainian diaspora have shifted their Christmas Eve meal to December 24. Or they celebrate both traditions.

In 2022, as a protest against the ongoing aggression by Russia, the Ukrainian government and Ukrainian Orthodox churches officially celebrated Christmas on December 25, symbolizing a move away from imperial influences and the churches' ties to the Russian Orthodox Church.

But no matter when Ukrainians celebrate Christmas or whether they'd immigrated to Canada a hundred years ago or last year, I can only imagine the relief they'd felt when they discovered that the mushrooms they'd harvested in the Ukraine for their Christmas celebrations also grew here.

Donna's family preserved the mushrooms they picked in the fall for their Christmas feast, unless, like in 2023, they were everywhere.

"Then I remember having the creamed mushrooms on rice with braised wild duck. My mother also dried some of the mushrooms and put them in potato soup. I also have some sliced and dehydrated that I use in a wild mushroom and chicken stew, and in wild rice and mushroom soup."

As time passed, it became Donna's job to provide the mushrooms: "When it became too difficult for my mother to walk on trails and through the bush, then I started to do the fall walks, looking for pidpanky so that we would have them for Christmas eve."

It's not that Donna isn't interested in mushrooms; she's just more interested in maintaining family traditions.

"I like going for the walks in the fall, and of course, foraging for free food seems to be endemic to Eastern European culture,"

Donna says. "And of course, you can't have Christmas Eve without these particular mushrooms."

But Donna is sixty-nine now and finds mushrooming more difficult than it used to be: "Ease of walking is getting harder each year so I tend to stay in accessible areas that don't involve contorting myself to crawl through the brush. As I follow the posts on the Mycological Society, I envy those on large properties that don't have far to go picking."

After several rounds of questions, Donna asked me a question: "And what is your connection with honey mushrooms?"

And I had to answer: "No connection."

But because I had been asking her intimate questions about how her family's traditions had been passed down and then passed around at Christmas dinner, I thought I owed her more. So I told her that three of my four grandparents were immigrants to Canada, from Ireland, Holland and Hungary. My Scottish grandfather was the third generation of his family to live in Canada. And there were no traditions of foraging for mushrooms in my family. There were what felt like no traditions at all, really, besides the mainstream holidays and traditions of the dominant Anglo-American culture, many of which seem to involve candy and sleeping in.

FINDING MY FIRST honey mushrooms was actually pretty easy.

Tom knew from his own experience – and from reports on WMS – that honeys had been spotted at Birds Hill Park. Once inside the park, it took another ten minutes to drive to the trail he wanted to use to walk into the woods proper and look for honeys.

Wood blewits (*Lepista nuda*), which are the faintest blue/lavender, were also on his list. They're both edible and for some reason, I hadn't ever gone looking for them. They just weren't on my radar: "eating mushrooms" is further down my list, after "finding and looking at any/every mushroom."

Tom is a great companion for foraging: he loves mushrooms as much as I do and he's more knowledgeable. I've got the eye, which means I spot lots of mushrooms, but I don't know everything about them. I'm okay with that as I get such pleasure from them and from simply being in the woods.

But it was very useful to have Tom walk me through the honey mushroom characteristics with a properly identified mushroom in hand. And it was sunny and warm and I got to play show and tell with Tom, which is the best game when it comes to mushrooming: "*Looooook* what I found!" Of course, most of the mushrooms I spotted were ones I knew, so I would be pointing out something and Tom would say, "Cool!" and then add "Um, that's a honey mushroom near your shoe."

IN THE WEEKS that followed my conversation with Donna, I couldn't stop thinking about my Irish granny, who'd come to Canada from County Wexford in 1922 when she was eleven years old, the youngest of six.

I don't remember anything particularly Irish about how she ran her household or the traditions she upheld. I don't know if she spoke the Irish language, otherwise known as Gaeilge, or even Yola, which was specific to Wexford, but if she did it was gone by the time I was around. I know she made glorious blueberry and banana cream pies, which she would serve at family dinners. We were loud and mean in our battles over pieces of those pies.

Because my parents shared a cabin in Minaki with my father's siblings, we didn't camp or travel, beyond the three hours' drive to northwestern Ontario. Though they enjoyed being outside, my parents were not people who were all that interested in the specifics of the outside.

But we did regularly pick wild blueberries. My mum used them in the pancakes she would make for us on weekend mornings on a griddle on the barbeque.

When she told stories about growing up in a Hungarian-Dutch household just outside Thunder Bay, my mum included those times they harvested rainbow smelt (*Osmerus mordax*) – which were introduced to Lake Superior in the early 1900s – in a stream behind her parents' rural property.

In both cases, these harvesting activities weren't cultural practices but grew out of local abundance. My grandparents had five children and ran a cattery and a kennel, which means there was a general hunger around their property.

And nothing beats wild blueberries. You can collect them in a bucket, into your shirt or even just jam handfuls directly into your mouth.

TOM AND I spent only a couple of sun-shot hours in Birds Hill Park but we found a million things, including an incredible haul of honeys once I got my eye in. Some of them were almost as big as pie plates!

But we also found: yellow/brown/black jelly fungus, wood ear mushrooms, puffballs, white bracket fungus with purple undersides (*Trichaptum biforme*) that had entirely covered a downed birch tree and an entirely new-to-me teal mushroom called green elf cups (*Chlorociboria aeruginascens*). The elf cup mycelia apparently stains the wood it grows on the same turquoise as the fruiting bodies and has been used in woodworking for centuries.

My favourite discovery was finding honey mushrooms tucked in tree branches. At first, I assumed that someone had walked there before us, but Tom and I soon realized that it was more likely that red squirrels were using the tree branches as a food dehydrator.

While honey mushrooms might dry slowly on tree branches, I knew from the posts on the WMS that they'd start to break down right away, even when kept in cloth bags in the fridge. I couldn't wait to process them, to get them in the food dehydrator and in a frying pan, like I could with the field mushrooms you get in the store.

It was dark by the time I'd completely filled up my dehydrator, which is satisfying in and of itself. A flatlay you can eat! I also cooked the honeys two ways: traditionally, with yogurt and dill, and then another batch flavoured with garlic, soy sauce and ginger. The hardest thing was only eating a little bit, which is a best practice with a new-to-you edible. Eat a mouthful, wait a day or even a day and a half to see if your belly reacts; if not, you can safely feast.

It was particularly hard this time: that mouthful was delicious!

The next day, as I waited to be able to eat a heaping bowl of honeys, I posted a macro picture of the green elf cups, which are the size/shape of a fingernail, albeit with a slightly wrinkled nailbed and a frilly edge.

And that social media post got the most comments of any of the hundreds of show-and-tell mushroom photos I have *ever* posted.

"Oh my goodness – I've never seen or imagined such a thing! Beautiful indeed," Anita Daher commented. PEI writer Carin Makuz added, "This is exactly how I imagine mushrooms looking should one be ON mushrooms." And poet Sheila Stewart wrote, "Teal hats!"

I will admit to being a bit indignant on behalf of the other, less flashy mushrooms.

THE HONEY MUSHROOM flush lasted only a few weeks.

But the strange weather continued, not just in Manitoba or even Canada, as David Phillips noted in his annual weather stories article: "The Earth's average temperature this summer was one for the record books. Moreover, 2023 is very likely to be the warmest year in possibly 125,000 years. For Canada, it was the warmest summer in 76 years, dating back to the start of national record-keeping in 1948."

Temperatures in June through November broke records globally.

In Canada, this resulted in record-breaking wildfire seasons in British Columbia, Alberta, Québec, Nova Scotia and the North-west Territories.

"184,493 square kilometres up in smoke across Canada – the equivalent of nearly 1.5 times the size of the Maritime Provinces," Philips wrote in his #1 weather story listing. "By June 27, Canada had already surpassed its historic record for total area burned but the country continued to burn."

After several years of wildfire smoke hanging over our cities and towns, Manitoba was one of the few places that wasn't smoked out in the summer of 2023.

But our weather was weird too.

Though we no longer regularly had snow by Hallowe'en – most of my childhood costumes were either half-covered by a winter coat or heavily insulated – that year snow fell on October 27.

And then it melted. All fall, the pattern was that a light skiff of snow would fall and then, a day or two later, would melt again, revealing green grass and a new flush of boulevard mushrooms.

There is a tree across the street from my house that always hosts colonies of velvet foot and ink cap mushrooms. In early November, I would walk over to see what had emerged overnight. One clump of velvet foots grew and got stepped on, grew and was collected by me for spore printing, grew and froze until

November 20, when a series of overnight frosts put an end to it. My favourite moment in this small pilgrimage was November 10, when the newly emerged mushrooms created a snowcave, lifting the thin carpet of snow and revealing both the mushrooms and the green grass beneath.

By mid-December 2023, it became clear that Manitoba – and probably the rest of Canada – would probably be having what's called a brown or even green Xmas, defined by Environment and Climate Change Canada as a Christian statutory holiday where there is less than two centimetres of snow on the ground.

Based on statistics going back to 1955, the chance of Winnipeg having a white Xmas are usually about 99 percent. The exceptions to the overwhelming rule, both in 1997 and this year, result from weather across Canada being affected by an El Niño system. And this year's El Niño is supercharged by climate change.

All of which meant that Manitoba, as well as other places in Canada, like the Rockies in BC and Alberta, southern Ontario and Quebec, had very little snow.

That's a problem because most of the country is already contending with severe drought. We need all the moisture we can get and we count on snow over the winter to provide that moisture, to replenish the water table.

NATALIIA HOLOVETSKA, HER husband, Roman, and her two teenage children are part of the wave of Ukrainian immigrants that came to Manitoba as a result of the Russia-Ukraine war that started in February 2022.

The war was in its 673rd day when I interviewed her in late December, thanks to an introduction from Anita Daher, who was one of many Manitobans who opened their homes to Ukrainian newcomers.

"We have been in Canada for one year and two months and we have not had the opportunity to pick mushrooms here," Nataliia said. In the Ukraine, her family regularly foraged for mushrooms. "My dad and my husband always went to the forest to pick various mushrooms at the end of the summer or at the beginning of fall. We lived in the west of Ukraine."

Nataliia sent me screen captures of pictures of the mushrooms that were common in their region and the dishes they cooked from them, all with Ukrainian-language labels.

As far as I could tell, in addition to honey mushrooms, her family foraged several kinds of boletes in addition to chanterelles. Nataliia said they dried them as well as cooking mushroom gravies and soups from fresh mushrooms. The division of labour was clear: her dad picked the mushrooms and her mom cooked and preserved them. But Nataliia's father died two years ago and her mother is back in Ukraine with the rest of the family, in the chaos and upheaval of war.

Nataliia said the reason they haven't gone mushrooming in Canada is twofold: First, they don't have much free time. Roman works long hours, even on Saturdays, and on Sundays they go to church. Second, they don't know where to pick in Manitoba.

When I asked if Roman missed mushrooming, Nataliia replied, "Oh yeah, a loooooot."

For Christmas Eve supper that year, Nataliia and Roman had found a big tub of dried wild mushrooms from Costco.

It wasn't perfect, but it was enough, especially given that many of the more than twenty-two thousand Ukrainian newcomers to Manitoba were struggling just before the holidays.

Winnipeg Free Press reporter Malak Abas wrote a series of stories about food security and inflation this fall. In early October, she reported on the 30 percent surge in food bank usage across Canada in 2023. And, for the first time, one in four Manitobans who used food banks had jobs. The most startling statistic came in late November: more than half of first-time food bank users at Harvest Manitoba were Ukrainian newcomers. Apparently, many of the Ukrainian newcomers – especially those with limited English – had struggled to find jobs, given the post-pandemic inflation belt-tightening that many companies/households were experiencing. Never mind the stress of war, of leaving home and trying to learn an entirely new place.

"Lots of folks that we spoke to during our surveying spoke about [how] they're not going home to anything, their home is no longer standing, their significant other or their partner might be still in Ukraine," Abas quoted Meaghan Erbus, director of network, advocacy and education for Harvest Manitoba, as saying. "So when they arrived in Manitoba, they had nothing. So they needed to start from fresh."

I AVIDLY LOOK for mushrooms now but don't remember seeing a single one in my childhood.

At the cabin, my sisters and I caught frogs and toads, garter snakes and crayfish. As we moved from the trees out onto the bare rock at the water's edge, we transitioned from pine needle–strewn moss to crunchy lichen.

One year, we scoured the broken rock of the shoreline for crayfish and collected enough for a crayfish boil, my parents knowing about the mercury in the watershed, from polluting pulp and paper mills, from industry, but reasoning that one feed wouldn't leave us with neurological damage.

Some of my most vivid memories are of the painted turtles napping in and amongst the low-slung blueberry bushes in Minaki. I remember chasing my younger sister back to our cabin with a painted turtle in my hands. I wanted to show her the turtle's painted belly but the turtle started to pee as soon as I picked it up, which is a defence mechanism, I believe, but my sister thought it was poison and started running, screaming at the top of her lungs.

I chased her with the peeing turtle held aloft, yelling, "Don't woooooooooooorry! It isn't poooooooooooison! It's just peeeeeeeeeeee."

One year, we picked blueberries to sell. I had a paper route and realized that besides the news of the world, I could probably also peddle wild blueberries to the people I delivered to. So my sister and I worked hard all weekend to pick a respectable amount of blueberries and Monday afternoon, I walked the neighbourhood, selling the slightly wizened blueberries by the cup from a box. My neighbours were bemused but they bought my blueberries like they were jewels, which in a way I suppose they were.

I don't know if my Irish granny learned how to make her excellent blueberry pie from the same wild blueberries in the Minaki patch my mother and I picked in. We have a picture of her as a youngish woman in Minaki and our cabin was apparently bought from some of her siblings, so it's possible.

IN LATE DECEMBER 2023, poet Brenda Sciberras was thinking of her mother, her grandparents and honey mushrooms.

Brenda Sciberras is a mix, like me. Her paternal grandparents immigrated to Winnipeg from Malta, while her maternal grandparents came from Ukraine to Vita, Manitoba, a Ukrainian enclave in southeast Manitoba founded in the 1890s.

When she was a child, Brenda and her mother, Stella, would travel to Vita to pick mushrooms with her grandparents Lena and Dmytro Prokipchuk, who Brenda knew as Baba and Gedo.

"In my early years, I would just carry the basket and follow along; later, I was set free in a specified area to fill my own basket, which was checked over later in the summer kitchen by Baba. My Gedo was the expert, so we only picked where he took us around the area. He knew the woods and pastures where pidpenky were plentiful."

Unlike Olga Kormilo, who only picked honey mushrooms, Gedo Dmytro's knowledge of mushrooms was more expansive – in the spring, they would also go looking for morels and something Brenda calls "orange caps," in addition to the fall harvest of honey mushrooms.

Brenda's mother and grandmother prepared creamed mushrooms. After the honey mushrooms were cleaned, which involved boiling/rinsing/draining them two times, they were cooked with butter, flour, garlic, onion, dill, parsley and cream. This dish was usually served alongside chicken or pork or with noodles or even perogies.

Though Brenda, now a mother and grandmother herself, doesn't go mushrooming anymore, her fondest memories involve her baba Lena's and then her mother's version of creamed mushrooms: "My mother would always ask what I wanted for my special birthday dinner. My answer was always, Baba's recipe for stewed pork with gravy, served with cornmeal and pidpenky."

"Mom always delivered," Brenda said, before noting that ninety-seven-year-old Stella had passed away in June. Brenda knew she'd miss her mother most when her January birthday rolled around.

LIKE BRENDA'S FATHER, Brassard married into a Ukrainian family: "My mother-in-law is Ukrainian, so I quickly realized that pidpenky is a revered, almost mythical species for that community. I understand the power of culinary traditions, the bounding ritual of family forays, and the iconic status of honey mushrooms . . .

but I'm a bit of a heretic. To me, they taste too strong and too chewy. I prefer the subtle, nutty flavours of our local porcini (*Boletus chippewaensis*), morels (*Morchella* sp.) and scotch bonnets (*Marasmius oreades*)."

Brassard is more interested in the biology of honey mushrooms than how they taste pickled or as a filling for pierogi.

"It's a 'badass' parasite that can decimate monoculture stands but can also help to diversify forest tree species," Brassard notes. "Its unique rhizomorphs can spread though great distance: there's an *Armillaria* growing in Oregon that's said to be the largest living organism on Earth. And oh, did I mention that *Armillaria*'s mycelium glows in the dark?"

Brassard is bristling with the kinds of ideas suitable to a founder: "Maybe the Winnipeg Mycological Society should advocate to make *Armillaria ostoyae* an official provincial symbol, along with white spruces, prairie crocuses and the Golden Boy . . ."

IN THE END, it snowed the day before Xmas 2023 in Winnipeg.

I now have an XL Ziploc bag of dark-brown dried honey mushrooms in my pantry that I haven't done anything with yet, though I bought and used dried mushrooms from a local forager.

Though it wasn't technically a brown Xmas, it was probably a rough holiday season for many of the Ukrainian newcomers and for everyone else who was struggling with inflated grocery prices.

I was grateful to have a bag full of food I got for free that I could afford to ignore for a few months.

A part of me wondered if I should have offered some of my honey mushroom bounty to Donna, Nataliia and Brenda. But I would have been asking them to rely on my Tom-supervised IDs of the mushrooms, which I was nervous about, after the fact. I had seen some WMS posts about toxic look-alikes emerging in honey mushroom clusters. I thought I was being pretty careful, but I didn't spore print every single mushroom.

Though most of my focus was on honey mushrooms as food, it's worth noting that Michael Kuo lists the deciduous tree–associated *Armillaria ostoyae*, one of two Manitoba species, as "a ravaging parasite feared by forest managers across the continent."

It feels strange now to be made so happy by a mushroom that kills trees. Though I feel no ambivalence about lobster mushrooms, which are the result of one fungi parasitizing another – strange/delicious! – I wonder, would I feel differently about Dutch elm disease, which is a fungal disease that kills elm trees, if it produced fruiting bodies I could eat?

I hope that the woods at Birds Hill Park survive this latest hot dry year, this latest drought, that they flourish despite it all. On that day in October, it certainly didn't look like the park's trees, shrubs and wildflowers were heat-stressed, but beyond the obvious signs of extreme drought I've seen – trees dropping yellowed leaves in August, stunted crops and withered-looking grasses and wildflowers – I'm not sure I'd know what to look for.

But I don't think that *not* picking honey mushrooms does anything to help the trees being parasitized by them. I decide that enjoying the picking and eating of a parasitic mushroom is similar to foraging for invasive species like garlic mustard in Ontario's forests. It's an adaptation, a climate change survival strategy of sorts.

I will also admit to some additional longing while doing my interviews, this time for the richness of Donna, Nataliia and Brenda's cultural traditions, even if some of them have fallen by the wayside over time. Sometimes I feel like all the cultural traditions I should have inherited from my immigrant grandparents have been stripped away, like a patch of blueberries where someone arrives the day before you do and not only takes the mature berries but the underripe ones too.

But that's not what matters: I knew my Irish granny and my Hungarian-Dutch mum loved me. I know they worked hard to make a safe place for me in their homes and in Canada. And that's all you can ask for, as a child and as an adult.

Also, after years finding mushrooms on my own, I've entered a much bigger room – a mush-room! – full of fun gals and fun guys like me. I've diversified my knowledge of fungi too. Some species are old friends, while I'm just getting to know others. And that's how it should be – I want to always keep learning, not just about mushrooms but about all the broken loveliness that is available to me as a resident of the Canadian prairies.

Acknowledgements

So, *Treed* was about trees and mushrooms while *Fungal* is about mushrooms and trees.

The main distinction between the two books, which I see as the first two parts of a three-book series, is that the five years I spent working on *Treed* were full of distress and chagrin. Though I had a journalism degree, a biology degree and twenty years' experience as a poet in addition to my love for trees, I didn't really know how to write science-y CNF, so I didn't finish a single essay for years, even though I had the wherewithal to start a new essay every three weeks.

I am so proud of where *Treed* wound up and the work it did in the world, but this time 'round, I couldn't help but be more relaxed. Even though I was writing *Fungal* during a global pandemic – in addition to all the catastrophic outcomes, it meant the research trips I had planned just weren't possible – I somehow felt more confident about the writing.

Partly, it was that I had a better idea of what I could do and what the form could stretch to accommodate, like a uterus.

Partly, it was that I had a great and helpful community of CNF writers: Yvonne Blomer, Tanis MacDonald, Ken Wilson, Kim Fahner, Kerry Ryan and Erna Buffie. Like me, all these writers work in a variety of genres. They were plastic: flexible but durable in their advice, in their friendship.

I am also part of a broader community of people who love books and art. So while my conversations with them aren't recorded in this book, I am grateful every day for Sue Sorensen,

Lauren Carter, Mitchell Toews, G.M.B. Chomichuk, Adele Perry, John Toews, Matthew Joudrey, Julie Kentner and Brenda Schmidt.

Poet Sally Ito and teacher Cherylene Kenter Hardie deserve special mention for their mudlarking companionship and cooperation. I have also appreciated spending time this way with poets Angeline Schellenberg and Joanne Epp.

Tom Nagy deserves special mention for somehow being my mushroom muse for this book. His knowledge and good humour are always much appreciated!

Residencies were important to me during the writing of this book. In spring 2021, I did a residency at the Buller Greenhouse at the University of Manitoba, thanks to MAC funding and the goodwill of Jo-Anne Joyce and Carla Dale. The Buller Greenhouse is one of my favourite places and I miss being able to dip into its humid airspace, being able to put down my stuff and go see what was blooming. (I never saw a mushroom there though!) I returned to UManitoba in winter 2022 as Writer-in-Residence at the Centre for Creative Writing and Oral Culture. I deeply appreciated the help/insight from CCWOC director/writer Jocelyn Thorpe and Mary Elliott. I am also grateful to St. John's College for providing an office so I had a different window to look out of.

I also spent two weeks in August 2022 at the Al Purdy A-frame in Ontario's Prince Edward County, Ontario, and all of March 2023 at Doris McCarthy Artist-in-Residence Centre in Scarborough, Ontario.

Other vital supports came from the Winnipeg Arts Council, the Manitoba Arts Council and the Canada Council for the Arts in these years. I don't think I could have written this book without their support – I was able to leave my permanent part-time job at University of Manitoba Press and concentrate on writing for a few years and I think that made all the difference.

I would like to thank Marijke Friesen, daughter-of-a-poet, brilliant graphic designer, for her work on this book.

I'd like to thank Noelle Allen at Wolsak & Wynn in two capacities. She was a smart and savvy editor, knowing exactly when to rein me in and what chunks of writing could be jettisoned. I am of the "if some is good, more MUST be better school," so this was an important role.

I trust Noelle implicitly, which says a lot for someone who has been in publishing a long time *and* who lives in the ambivalence produced by urban ecosystems in a time of climate change. She's also an excellent publisher and a leader among independent publishers. I would follow her anywhere (with a battered suitcase full of manuscripts needing a home).

I'd also like to thank Hollay Ghadery for all her promo wizardry. I *so* appreciate the time and energy she spent on *Fungal*, especially given her own writing practice. She's so good! Hire/ publish her if you can!

Thanks too to the rest of the team at W&W: Jason Allen, Ashley Hisson, Jennifer Rawlinson and especially Jen Hale for her wise/perceptive/funny copy edit. It has been a pleasure to work with you!

I am so proud of my daughter, Anna, who she is now and who she will be. And I am so grateful to my partner Michael for twenty-five years of foolishness. I like to say that my little Irish granny set me up with workingman's tea but it was Michael who introduced me to Assiniboine Forest, where I first learned to love fungi.

Notes

Mushroom Tourist

I began this book where I began my mushrooming, in Winnipeg's Assiniboine Forest, one of the only spaces in Winnipeg that hasn't been developed. I wanted to show the things that would be available to someone most days and most seasons in the forest. I am a professional noticer, but once you begin to pay attention to the world, to the urban ecosystem, there's lots to see. I think being in relationship with the more-than-human means that we understand that we're not alone in this world, that we have a responsibility to these organisms and to the land we all inhabit.

I am proud to live on Treaty 1 territory, the ancestral territory of the Anishinaabe, Cree, Dakota and Oji-Cree peoples and the homeland of the Métis Nation.

Mushrooming

A version of this essay first appeared on Kerry Clare's blog, *Pickle Me This*. It was a follow-up to my essay "Primipara," which appeared in Clare's anthology, *The M Word: Conversations about Motherhood*. Kerry is a firecracker in a nice dress! A version closer to the one that appears here was published in *Canthius* magazine in winter 2023.

My daughter, Anna, who will turn eighteen a few days after this book is launched, consented to her appearance in this and all the other essays in this book.

Red River Mushroomer

When I worked at *Prairie Fire* magazine in my very early twenties, one of my jobs was to open the mail. Since this was how all submissions came in, I saw the good and bad. My favourite submissions were centred God poems from jail. I wrote the shape poems in the two mudlarking / mushroom essays independently from the essays but immediately saw their potential to be jammed into them. I will acknowledge Jenna Butler and Tanis MacDonald as very good models for this behaviour and Noelle for understanding that poets – even poets writing prose – can't always help themselves.

Harvester

My thanks to Jonathan Stevens, of Jonathan's Farm, for letting me haul onions and clean garlic in September 2020, even though I was slow and creaky. And possibly mouthy. I love getting my veg, through the growing season, from Jonathan's Farm and his CSA. I love the farmers' market they've set up around the CSA pickup, especially as they provided a venue for me to launch *Pandemic Papers*, my draw-write collab with Natalie Baird that At Bay Press published. In August 2020, it was the only venue we could find!

In order to protect their privacy, I have changed the names of my Loveday co-workers.

Cultivator

This essay appeared in *Canadian Notes & Queries* in fall 2022. It had its first, spore-filled airing at the Association of Literature, Environment and Culture in Canada (or ALECC) conference in June 2022. I have relied on the ALECC and *The Goose*, the e-journal it produces, for all my lit/environmental conversation for more than a decade. But at that moment, I felt reassured that the weird/smelly/mushroomy things I was writing worked for other people too . . .

In the Kitschen

When you say, publicly, that you like *something*, people get you versions of that *thing* for years. Friends once made the mistake of saying they particularly liked turtles or elephants and then, somehow, they had a sizable collection of figurines/books/stickers/stuffies. For years, I loved mushrooms but loved/hated mushroom kitsch, which is why I had to write this essay. I have since reconciled myself.

Morel Hunter

I think the reason I like morels so much – besides how tasty they are – is that they continue to confound me. Here's to finding my own morel patch, deep in Crown land! (Tom, want to go morel-picking?)

Red River Mudlarker

This essay was second-place winner of the 2022 Kloppenburg Hybrid *Grain* Contest in Regina's *Grain* magazine, as selected by Liz Howard. Forcing someone as good as Howard to read/comment on my work was the best reward, though I still deposited the award cheque.

Eating My Words

I knew if I didn't write about psilocybin or magic mushrooms, if I didn't address it in some way, I would be side-eyed. My thanks to my writer-friend, who shared his journey from antidepressants to microdoses of psilocybin and to therapist Celeste Seiferling, who helped me to think through taking/not taking magic mushrooms. And thanks to Tom for making me a bookshroom!

Rotten

This essay was published by Calgary's *FreeFall* magazine in spring 2023. My thanks to Micheline Maylor, Crystal Mackenzie and the rest of the *FF* team. In early March 2024, I got word that it was selected by editor Emily Urquhart (who I greatly admire) for *Best Canadian Essays 2025*, which will be published by Biblioasis in fall 2024. I am looking forward to seeing that essay fruit on another stump!

In case anyone is worried: I tested negative for cervical cancer and have continued to test negative in successive colposcopies. I am grateful to Dr. Carrie Corbett, obstetrician gynecologist, for her good and thoughtful care and, also, for laughing at my jokes. My boulevard elm's first test for DED was inconclusive and then definitive: it was cut down in July 2023 and has not been replaced. I *may* have seeded the mulch-filled hole with velvet foots and ink caps. I am thinking a linden or a silver maple might be a nice replacement but, honestly, I will be happy with any tree.

Fun Gal

I would like to thank the Punter and Lamont families for their generosity of spirit and for the mushroomy inheritance. Though I can't hope to match David's efforts, I like to think I am a fun gal of sorts. Thanks, too, to the University of Manitoba's Archives & Special Collections, which resides in the Elizabeth Dafoe Library, for housing and sharing David Punter's papers. Archivists are the best!

Pidpanky Picker

I am grateful to everyone for sharing their family stories about honey mushrooms, about tradition, time and knowledge transfer. Now I want to go blueberry picking! And I so appreciate Alexandre Brassard and his team of experts for their work on the Winnipeg Mycological Society/Société mycologique de Winnipeg group on Facebook. For the first time, I am not alone in my love of mushrooms!

ARIEL GORDON (she/her) is a Winnipeg/Treaty 1 Territory-based writer, editor and enthusiast. She is the ringleader of Writes of Spring, a National Poetry Month project with the Winnipeg International Writers Festival that appears in the *Free Press* and will celebrate its tenth birthday in 2025. Gordon is also the poetry editor of *The Goose*. In 2019, Wolsak & Wynn published *Treed: Walking in Canada's Urban Forests*. It received an honourable mention for the 2020 Alanna Bondar Memorial Book Prize for environmental humanities and creative writing from ALECC and was shortlisted for the Carol Shields Winnipeg Book Award. Gordon's most recent book is *Siteseeing: Writing nature & climate across the prairies*, written in collaboration with Saskatchewan poet Brenda Schmidt and published in fall 2023 by Winnipeg's At Bay Press. It was nominated for a 2024 Saskatchewan Book Award in the poetry category.